LANGUAGE OF THE ROBE

LANGUAGE
OF THE ROBE
AMERICAN INDIAN TRADE BLANKETS

ROBERT W. KAPOUN

WITH

CHARLES J. LOHRMANN

GIBBS·SMITH PUBLISHER

PEREGRINE SMITH BOOKS

SALT LAKE CITY

First paperback edition 1997

00 99 98 97   3 2 1

Text and color photographs copyright © 1992 by Robert W. Kapoun

This is a Peregrine Smith book, published by

Gibbs Smith, Publisher

P.O. Box 667

Layton, Utah 84041

Design by Clarkson Creative

All color photographs by Lynn Lown unless otherwise noted

Printed and bound in Hong Kong

Library of Congress Cataloging-in-Publication Data

Language of the robe : American Indian trade blankets / Robert W.
Kapoun with Charles J. Lohrmann.

p. cm.

"Peregrine Smith book"–T.p. verso.

Includes bibliographical references.

ISBN 0-87905-468-9 (hardcover). – ISBN 0-87905-811-0 (pbk.)

1. Indians of North America–Costume.

2. Indian textile fabrics–North America.

3. Blankets–North America. I. Lohrmann, Charles J.

[E98.C8K36 1997]

391'.008997–dc21   96-44485

CIP

CONTENTS

ANGRY

FOREWORD

Much of what we know about traditional Native American clothing and costume is derived from our knowledge and interpretation of these same artifacts in our own culture. That is, we have applied to the Native American our own personal and cultural experience in acquiring, tailoring, and wearing a variety of garments.

Something of this can be seen, for example, in *Robes of White Shell and Sunrise*, the Denver Art Museum's acclaimed 1974 catalogue of the "Personal Decorative Arts of the Native American." In it, Richard Conn, the author/curator, organized the text and the exhibit which accompanied it into categories that illustrate the reliance we have on the perception of clothing in our own culture.

At the core of this work are four chapters entitled, "Wrapped and Folded Clothing," "Binary Clothing," "Fitted Clothing," and "The Crowning Touch" (headgear). Each of these descriptive titles is derived from a western fashion or tailoring concept; and while this catalogue is most informative, its basic orientation to clothing and costume is non-Indian, despite its restriction to Native American artifacts.

Unquestionably, a larger appreciation of the Native American clothing and costume must include an "insider's" view. In fact, one could argue that, without a participant's understanding of what he or she wears, descriptions of any foreign culture's dress are incomplete or even misleading. To gain this "insider's" knowledge, the frames of reference about clothing and costume as Westerners know them must be replaced, or at least blurred. Clothing, whether male or female, cannot be labeled and studied simply as material culture. Its realm is dynamic and synergistic, alternating within and between the sacred and the profane.

The subject of this book, *Language of the Robe*, is a case in point. First created by Europeans and later American manufacturers, this western garment was recast by its Native American users to meet the needs and acceptance of these new owners. Curiously, no treatment of trade blankets was presented in *Robes of White Shell and Sunrise*, ostensibly because they are non-Indian in origin and manufacture. Yet, the trade blanket and other manufactured cloth and "yard goods" were among the earliest of exchange items among and between Native Americans and Europeans. As testimony to the importance of the trade blanket, its adoption and use by Native Americans encompassed this entire continent.

A large segment of the literature about the American Indian trade blanket as garment is based on our knowledge of similar costuming indigenous to the Great Plains and the American Southwest. That is, we see in the machine-woven American Indian trade blankets the historic replacement of the painted buffalo robe of the Plains and the hand-loomed striped blanket designed and created by the Navajo and Pueblo weavers.

There are, however, a variety of issues about the Plains buffalo robe and the Southwest's wearing blanket that have been lost in our application and translation of their use and aesthetics to the trade blanket. Clearly, two of the areas of neglect which merit further study relate to the cultural communication inherent in the ways people wear clothing and costume as well as the philosophical dimensions of them. For example, we can take a look at what ideas or emotions the American Indian people communicate when they wear the trade blanket.

A study in point concerning cultural communications through the use of the wearing blanket is seen in the Omaha ethnography by Alice Fletcher and Francis La Flesche. Hidden within volume 27 of the BAE Annual Report for 1905–1906 is a description of the nonverbal communication practiced in the past on the Southern Plains using the buffalo robe. At the turn of the century, when the photography for this publication was done, it was necessary to

HESITATION

OLD MAN WALKING

WALKING

COURTSHIP

substitute a trade blanket for a robe. Nonetheless, the phenomenon described therein as "the language of the robe" depicts the use of the substitute blanket as a means of communication.

Of the nine poses shown, only three are linked to specific messages: "hesitation," "admonition," and "anger." The other six gestures describe states of being. For example, one plate (53C) illustrates the following:

"Now the man is addressing the tribe or council. The moment waited for has arrived and he steps forth to speak his thought, to impress his views upon his tribesmen."[1]

In addition, the "language of the robe" shown here and described by Fletcher and La Flesche is gender-specific to Omaha males. Yet there is some hint that a similar language was available to women and their robes in the authors' statement:

There still lives in the memory of one of the writers a June day nearly thirty years ago when an Omaha girl was seen flitting among the tall prairie flowers, shifting her white blanket to suit her varying moods—now gathering it about her slight, swaying figure, now letting it float as she swept in ever-widening curves, or at the slightest sound, hiding her glossy head and laughing face among its soft folds.[2]

What seems obvious from the Omaha study is the fact that on the Plains, the buffalo robe and later the trade blanket were important devices or props in the communication of subtle ideas or emotions. This communication was achieved by the different ways the blanket was worn—all without uttering a sound.

At a different level is the importance of tribal mythology in the explanation of designs woven into textiles by the native people of the Southwest. In this regard, a clue to one of the earliest Navajo wearing blanket designs, the so-called First Phase Chief's blanket, is possibly explained by oral traditions which link the wearing blanket to modes of transportation by supernatural beings. For example, Gladys A. Reichard, in her book *Navajo Religion*, relates the story of the Twins being given rainbows to keep in the folds of their blankets. Rainbows and lightning are for the Navajo two of the most important means of travel by sacred personages across the *dinetah* (the Navajo world).[3]

As woven by the Navajo artisans, First Phase Chief's blankets have stripes of white, brown, blue, and, on occasion, red. It seems quite possible to view these stripes as metaphors for the Twins aerial color, avenues of travel held in the folds of every Navajo's blanket—at least at one point in time. Still, in the realm of philosophy or poetic metaphor, the French philosopher Gaston Bachelard suggests a new way of seeing blankets, Native American or other. Blankets expound the aesthetic of a "drape." Quite simply, blankets

ADDRESSING THE TRIBE

ADMONITION

RUNNING

WATCHING

make us round.

Bachelard, in "The Phenomenology of Roundness," the last chapter in *The Poetics of Space*, quotes the Dutch artist van Gogh as saying, "Life is probably round."[4] Also the German philosopher, Karl Jaspers, is cited with the thought that "every being seems in itself round." Obviously, the shape of one's body is smoothed and swelled by wearing a blanket, and this harmony creates beauty on several levels.

Yet what are we to make of the "addiction" of Native Americans for the Indian trade blanket? Certainly blankets keep one warm. And blankets are the visual clue for lovers in Plains pictorial art; but surely there is more to its success than these bodily comforts.

It seems to me that in the pages that follow the reader should look for the magic in the American Indian trade blanket—the same magic that wearers saw and felt when cocooned within them. The blanket is a poetic statement given voice by the wearer. The meaning of these poetic statements are as varied as there are audiences who hear them. For me, I hear van Gogh: "Life is probably round."

PATRICK T. HOULIHAN
**DIRECTOR, MILLICENT A. ROGERS MEMORIAL MUSEUM,
TAOS, NEW MEXICO**

BIBLIOGRAPHY

1. Fletcher, Alice, and Francis La Flesche. *The Omaha Tribe.* Washington, D.C.: Bureau of American Ethnology, no. 27. 1905–1906, p. 362.

2. Ibid., p. 360.

3. Gladys A. Reichard. *Navajo Religion: A Study of Symbolism* (Tucson: University of Arizona Press, 1983).

4. Bachelard, Gaston. *The Poetics of Space.* Boston: Beacon Paper, 1969.
For further reference:
Conn, Richard. *Robes of White Shell and Sunrise.* Denver: Denver Art Museum, 1974.

PREFACE

There are three questions that I am asked more often than any others concerning the American Indian trade blankets. They are:

1. What is an American Indian trade blanket?
2. How did you start collecting these blankets?
3. How do you find these blankets?

The answers to these questions explain all the reasons why we wanted to collect the trade blankets.

What is an American Indian trade blanket? In the simplest terms, an American Indian trade blanket is a commercially created, machine-woven wearing blanket produced for an American Indian market. Even though the following pages tell the history of the trade blanket, it is important to state that, prior to the production of these blankets, the Indian people were able to provide warmth for themselves by relying on native or natural means. Historically, wearing robes were created from animal hides and fur, woven plant fibers, and, ultimately, fabric woven by hand from wool or cotton. With European contact and the introduction of trade goods, suddenly the need for these traditional forms of protective clothing was altered. The trade blanket replaced the hide robes and hand-woven blankets previously worn by native people. The development of a market for these blankets parallels the evolution of the Indian people's cultural existence.

How did you start collecting these blankets? The answer to the second question requires a more detailed response. My wife, Marianne, and I have been very fortunate to own an American Indian art gallery, The Rainbow Man, in Santa Fe, New Mexico. This has allowed us the opportunity to become familiar with the Rio Grande Pueblo people, their dances and their customs. It was at these dances that our love affair with the trade blankets was kindled.

Watch any Pueblo dance, whether in the summer or in the winter, and you will see trade blankets being worn or used. Look at the Indian women watching the dance and you'll see that every one of them is wearing a brightly colored shawl. Watch the men singing, dancing, or drumming, and often you'll see blankets being used as part of their attire. These blankets are not merely being worn to provide warmth; they create a statement, if you will, which says, "These blankets are part of our culture."

The blanket alone makes more of a visual statement of "Indianness" than any other item. This statement holds true throughout all of the Indian cultures, from the Plains and Plateau people to the tribes of the Northwest Coast. The inherent beauty that these blankets have, and their importance to the Indian people are the two main reasons we decided to collect the American Indian trade blankets.

How do you find these blankets? This question is the most difficult to answer. Before we could collect the blankets, we first had to learn their history. We started buying the most recent blankets produced by Pendleton Woolen Mills, which is the only major manufacturer of an Indian-design blanket on the market today. But very soon, we were buying blankets that we couldn't identify as Pendleton blankets. Since no one could tell us what we had, we started to pursue answers on our own. With every new discovery, we found that we were making the puzzle larger instead of finding pieces that would solve our original puzzle.

Even though I feel confident that we have a good understanding of the history of these blankets, you'll note we've included a chapter on blankets of unknown origin. I'm hoping that, as soon as this book is published, these "unknowns" will become known.

It is also my hope that this book will stimulate further research on the American Indian trade blanket.

ROBERT W. KAPOUN

ACKNOWLEDGEMENTS

No one walks a path that either hasn't been walked before, or who hasn't needed help from others to walk that path. I'd like to thank my wife, Marianne, not only for walking that path with me, but also for helping me be able to make that walk. Our pursuit of the American Indian trade blankets has been a shared vision.

A special word of thanks is extended to the American Indian people. They can certainly claim to be the first to value and collect the trade blankets. My thanks go out to Angie Reano Owen and her family of Santo Domingo Pueblo. Thank you for allowing me to share some of your world. My understanding of the true importance of these blankets in your lives has been the inspiration to write this book.

Finally, to all the people who have made this work possible, I sincerely thank you.

INDIAN WOMAN AND CHILD, C. 1910. THIS WAY OF
CARRYING INFANTS IS STILL PRACTICED TODAY AMONG
MOST NATIVE AMERICANS, ESPECIALLY THE PUEBLO PEOPLE.
(PHOTO BY WILL PENNINGTON, COURTESY BOB KAPOUN)

SECTION ONE
THE HUMANIST PERSPECTIVE ON
THE TRADE BLANKET

THE NATIVE AMERICAN PERSPECTIVE ON THE TRADE BLANKET

A WOMAN'S EXPERIENCE
BY RAIN PARRISH

WHEN I WAS A CHILD, MY FAMILY ATTENDED SACRED NAVAJO CEREMONIES AND DANCES. I REMEMBER STARRY NIGHTS AFTER THE FIRST FROST, WHEN THE SEASON OF STORYTELLING BEGAN AND THE YEI-BEI-CHAIS WERE TO ARRIVE. WE LOADED MY FATHER'S TRUCK WITH FOOD, PENDLETON BLANKETS, AND QUILTS, AS WE PREPARED TO SPEND THE NIGHTS AT THE SITE OF THE UPCOMING CEREMONY. MY MOTHER DRESSED US IN BEAUTIFUL CLOTHES SHE HAD MADE HERSELF—VELVET BLOUSES WITH SILVER BUTTONS AND LONG SKIRTS. THE PEOPLE TRAVELED BY HORSE-DRAWN COVERED WAGONS OR IN TRUCKS. WHEN WE ARRIVED AT THE CEREMONIAL SITE, THERE WAS ALWAYS THE SMELL OF PIÑON AND CEDAR SMOKE IN THE AIR. THIS SCENT, MIXED WITH THE AROMA OF ROASTING LAMB, LET ME KNOW THIS WAS A SPECIAL OCCASION. • ALONG WITH THE DISTINCTIVE SMELLS, THERE WAS THE SOUND OF BLEATING SHEEP MIXING WITH THE TALKING AND QUIET LAUGHTER OF THE PEOPLE SETTING UP CAMP. THESE OCCASIONS WERE ALL ABOUT RENEWING FAMILY RELATION-SHIPS, SO AFTER WE SET UP OUR CAMP, WE FOUND PLACES NEAR THE CENTRAL FIRE TO HEAR THE MEN SING THE RELIGIOUS OR SOCIAL SONGS REQUIRED BY THE PARTICULAR CEREMONY. • ALL AROUND WERE MEN, WOMEN, AND CHILDREN DRESSED IN THEIR FINEST VELVET, SATIN, OR COT-TON PRINT CLOTHES. THERE WAS THE GLINT OF SILVER JEWELRY ACCENTS. AND THEY WERE always wrapped in Pendleton blankets.

We watched the young men and women dance together in a circle, their bodies draped together with a blanket. I can still see the big black hats with silver hatbands and colored scarves over long black hair (tsiiyeel) bundled back with brightly colored yarns.

As the light from the fire illuminated the moving bodies and blankets, the swirling shapes, lines, patterns and colors sprang to life. I no longer saw blankets, but rather the familiar designs of the Holy People coming to life from the sand paintings. I saw moving clouds, glowing sunsets, varicolored streaks of lightning, rainbow goddesses, sacred mountains, horned toads and images like desert mirages—all dancing before my eyes.

Another colorful community occasion was the trip to the trading post with my parents. This was always a special social event. I remember looking for the small truck that delivered letters and parcels. Often, the truck also provided transportation for the people who were returning home from trips away from the reservation. The trading post was always crowded with people who had come to shop, trade and enjoy the social event. There was joy and excitement among those gathered at the post. The counters were lined with people wearing their colorful clothing and blankets. The shelves were stocked with clothing, food, saddles, bridles, and cooking utensils. And Pendleton blankets.

Women traded their hand-woven rugs for goods like flour, salt, sugar, vegetables, and coffee. There were cotton prints and velvet fabrics in assorted colors for making skirts and blouses. As a special reward to herself for her hard work, or as a special gift for someone else, the Navajo woman had the pleasure of buying a colorful Pendleton robe or shawl. Only she knew the many hours of back-breaking labor she had devoted to herding sheep and preparing and processing the sheep wool to spin yarn needed for weaving. After weeks or even months of painstaking work, she would complete the weaving that possessed qualities of balance, rhythm, and harmony. And a trade blanket was part of the valuable reward for that work.

It was said that our world was created by Father Sky and Mother Earth a very long time ago. Their child was Changing Woman, our revered female deity, who created the Navajo people, the plants, and the animals. Changing Woman shared the story of the Blessingway, which became our religious ceremony. Men and women learned the philosophy and understood the meaning of the word *hozhooji*, "on the side of beauty." Our families knew what it meant to create beautiful things like silver work, baskets, sand paintings, and music to accompany our healing ceremonies. We were taught to believe in a world view in which harmony, success, order, blessedness, and beauty were paramount.

The words and chants of the Blessingway enclose the nature of Navajo thought and express the integration of all aspects of existence into a harmonious whole. They instruct us on how to live and celebrate our daily life, from childhood through old age. We were taught how to summon and embrace well-being and prosperity for one another and, in turn, present offerings to Mother Earth and Father Sky.

And so, with each new beginning, we honor our rite of passage with gifts of fabrics and jewels (or soft and hard goods). Always, as we move through any phase in our lives, we sprinkle cornmeal and pollen to insure that we might lead a long and happy life. And colorful blankets are often the chosen gift. We welcome our children with a handmade quilt or a small Pendleton blanket as we wrap them in our prayers. For our young men and women, we celebrate the transforma-tion into adulthood, by discipline, values, acknowledgement, and gifts. As they lie on a thick bed of Pendleton blankets, we massage their bodies for good health. For a couple's marriage, we share wisdom and a feast that includes cornmeal mush. To honor the occasion, the woman's body is draped with a Pendleton shawl, the man's with a Pendleton robe.

As we move into old age, we pay tribute to the spirit world with ceremony, prayers, and gifts. Often we bury our people with their special possessions and beautiful Pendleton blankets.

Rain Parrish is of Navajo descent. She is a former curator at Santa Fe's Wheelwright Museum and is currently a freelance writer in Santa Fe.

A MAN'S EXPERIENCE
BY BOB BLOCK

A blanket is an extension of an Indian man's status and feelings.

In the past, an Indian man judged wealth and status in numbers of horses. Today, trade blankets are like horses were in past times. They define a person's means and are a part of his personal wealth. For example, if a man's daughter is chosen to be a princess for a gathering or a powwow, he shows his appreciation by giving trade blankets to the people who bestowed this honor on his daughter.

Friendship is highly important to an Indian man. A gift of a trade blanket is the best way for him to express his feelings of friendship and his appreciation for a good friend. The giving of a blanket is of such importance that an Indian man will ask another man to speak for

MARCIELO QUINTANA, COCHITI PUEBLO, C. 1920. BLANKETED FOR MAXIMUM WARMTH AND PROTECTION FROM THE ELEMENTS. (PHOTO BY T. HARMON PARKHURST, COURTESY MUSEUM OF NEW MEXICO, NEG.43734)

him. The honored spokesman is someone for whom the man has respect and feelings of empathy. The spokesman is chosen because he has a strong feeling for the words that will convey the intention of the presentation.

A trade blanket might appeal to an Indian man because of his personal preference for its color and design. He will purchase the blanket or trade for it and it will become one of his favorites. He'll store it in a cedar chest and bring it out for special occasions or as a gift for someone he respects deeply.

When a man receives a trade blanket as a gift from a special person—his grandmother, uncle, wife, or an elder man—he will consider this blanket above all other blankets. This most significant blanket will be used for special occasions, such as tribal ceremonies, dances, weddings, or deaths. This special blanket will not be given away but will be kept and honored for the man's entire life.

I remember when my great-aunt, one of the original Osage allottees, wanted me to be inducted into our traditional Osage dances—the *In-lon-schka*. She commissioned my entire dance outfit to be made. Then, as a part of her gift, she gave me one of her special trade blankets. I will always keep and honor this blanket because it has a special place in my heart and reminds me of my great-aunt.

Dances are traditional and are held for four days—Thursday through Sunday—in the summer of each year. On Sunday, the fourth day, the Giveaway is held. Friends and relatives of Osages are honored with individual songs, and they dance on these songs.

After the song, they give money, trade blankets, shawls, and groceries.

A blanket is the most prized gift, and it is given for special reasons. A blanket is given to express appreciation for someone who has come from afar to attend the dances. Or, a blanket might be given to a person or a family who has shown kindness in hard times or in times of sorrow over a lost loved one. And trade blankets are also given to acknowledge someone for his or her efforts in the business world or in the religious community.

When I was accepted by the head committeeman of the village to become a member of the Osage *In-lon-schka* dances, the town crier announced my entry into the dance arena by calling my Osage name. Then, I entered the arena with the town crier and my great-aunt. The head man placed my eagle feather in the roach top piece on my head and told the people my name and the reason the name was given.

Then, by my instructions, the head man would speak for me, and ask the drum keepers of each village to come forward. As each one came forward, I draped a trade blanket on his shoulders. I then asked for the town crier to come forward and I gave him a blanket and some money. Then, after I draped a blanket on the head man, I walked out to the drum in the middle of the dance arena and placed money for the singers on the drum.

After all these gifts were given, the whip man took me to the seat that was designated for me. I put my blanket down on the seat and then officially became part of the dances. This giving of gifts—the Giveaway—is called paying for the honor to dance and giving thanks for this honor.

Just as giving the gift of a trade blanket is important, the receiving of a blanket is another show of acceptance within the Indian community. I have vivid memories of the first time I danced. On Sunday, one of the most respected elders of the tribe gave me a blanket. I felt like I was then an integral part of the occasion. I was accepted and appreciated for participating in our tribal dances. I was accepted among our people. I still respect this feeling, and I will hold it dear for all of my life.

A few years later, another respected elder man gave me a trade blanket during the Giveaway on Sunday. Even though this gift of a blanket was done without the spoken word, the gift affirmed that I was on the right path and was part of the tribe. The knowledge that I was a part of the tribe and resulting feeling of unity with others has encouraged me. When I go out into the world, I know I have a foundation of support among my people. I will always remember this act of appreciation by the elder men. It is understood.

Bob Block is of Osage descent and is an active member of the Osage community.

A HISTORIC PERSPECTIVE ON THE BLANKET
BY LUTHER STANDING BEAR
from his autobiography, Land of the Spotted Eagle (1933)

According to the white man, the Indian, choosing to return to his tribal manners and dress, "goes back to the blanket." True, but "going back to the blanket" is the factor that has saved him from, or at least stayed, his final destruction. Had the Indian been as completely subdued in spirit as he was in body he would have perished within the century of his subjection. But it is the unquenchable spirit that has saved him—his clinging to Indian ways, Indian thought, and tradition, that has kept him and is keeping him today. The white man's ways were not his ways and many of the things that he has tried to adopt have proven disastrous and to his utter shame. Could the Indian have forestalled the flattery and deceit of his European subjector and retained his native truth and honesty; could he have shunned whiskey and disease and remained the paragon of health and strength he was, he might today be a recognized man instead of a hostage on a reservation. But many an Indian has accomplished his own personal salvation by "going back to the blanket." The Indian blanket or buffalo robe, a true American garment, and worn with the significance of language, covered beneath it, in the prototype of the American Indian, one of the bravest attempts ever made by man on this continent to rise to the heights of true humanity.

To clothe a man falsely is only to distress his spirit and to make him incongruous and ridiculous, and my entreaty to the American Indian is to retain his tribal dress.

SAN ILDEFONSO PUEBLO MAN, C. 1935, WEARING A
STRIPED BLANKET POPULAR WITH MOST INDIAN PEOPLE.
(PHOTO BY T. HARMON PARKHURST, COURTESY
MUSEUM OF NEW MEXICO, NEG. 55202)

THE LANGUAGE OF THE ROBE

BY CHARLES J. LOHRMANN

OVER THE MANY GENERATIONS SINCE NATIVE AMERICANS BEGAN TRADE WITH EUROPEANS, FEW ITEMS HAVE BECOME SO CLOSELY IDENTIFIED WITH THE INDIGENOUS AMERICAN CULTURES—PARTICULARLY THOSE OF THE PLAINS AND THE SOUTHWEST—AS HAS THE AMERICAN INDIAN TRADE BLANKET. IN FACT, BECAUSE THE COLORFUL WEARING ROBE OR TRADE BLANKET HAS BECOME SUCH AN INTEGRAL PART OF THE CULTURES OF MANY AMERICAN INDIAN TRIBES, TRADE BLANKETS ARE ALMOST UNIVERSALLY KNOWN AS "INDIAN BLANKETS." • EVEN THOUGH THE TERM "INDIAN BLANKET" IS MISLEADING IN THE SENSE THAT THE ORIGIN OF THE TRADE BLANKET ITSELF WAS FROM OUTSIDE THE NATIVE CULTURES, THE TERM IS APPROPRIATE BECAUSE THE TRADE BLANKET HAS BECOME ALMOST COMPLETELY RECONTEXTUALIZED IN TERMS OF NATIVE CULTURES. AS PATRICK HOULIHAN SAYS IN HIS FOREWORD TO THIS BOOK, THE TRADE BLANKET IS AN OBJECT TAKEN FROM THE WHITE CULTURE AND "RECAST BY ITS NATIVE AMERICAN USERS." IN OTHER WORDS, EVEN THOUGH THE TRADE BLANKET ORIGINATED OUTSIDE THE NATIVE AMERICAN CULTURES, IT TOOK THE PLACE OF HAND-LOOMED TEXTILES AND BUFFALO OR OTHER ROBES OF NATIVE MATERIALS FOR BOTH CEREMONIAL AND PRACTICAL USES. ONCE THE TRADE BLANKET WAS MORE WIDELY ACCEPTED, IT WAS ALSO DESCRIBED BY THE WORD *ROBE*, A TERM PREVIOUSLY used only for animal hide "blankets." Robe was also used later by the major trade blanket manufacturers to describe the wearing blankets sold to the non-Indian market. No doubt, *robe* was a more successful advertising term as it evokes a more poetic image, but it is also more accurate, as it implies the blanket was to be draped over the shoulders or wrapped around a figure, rather than just used as bedding.

On first consideration, the obvious importance of the trade blanket is the practical—the robe provides warmth and protection against the elements. Before the introduction of the commercially produced blanket through trade with Europeans, the creation of the robe varied with the natural materials available to each particular tribe. As the original material for the blanket or robe varied, so did the specific cultural importance. But the robe—whether fur, bark, feather, or woolen—has long held an important place in the lifeways of many Native American people.

European accounts of the use of robes by Indian people date back to the earliest contact between the two worlds. In 1673, when French explorers Louis Joliet and Jesuit Father Jacques Marquette traveled along the Mississippi River, they first encountered bison and noted that "the body is covered with a heavy coat of curly hair... it falls off in the summer, and the skin becomes as soft as velvet. At that season, the savages use the hides for making fine robes, which they paint in various colors."[1]

When Meriwether Lewis and William Clark, during their landmark expedition to chart the lands acquired by the United States in the Louisiana Purchase, made contact with the Otoes in 1804, it was noted that "the men were almost naked, wearing only a breechcloth and loose blanket or buffalo robe, painted."[2]

In a history of tribes of the Northwest, Colonel O. G. Shields describes a variety of native blankets, including those of "the Nez Perces and other tribes in the Fraser-Columbia area [who] were extremely skillful in producing heavy and tastefully decorated blankets in twined weaving from mountain goat's hair with warp of vegetal fiber." These and other native blankets "were the groundwork of great skill and taste and much mythology, and were decorated with strips of fur, fringes, tassels, pendants, beadwork, featherwork, and native money."[3]

In the Southwest, Shields notes that the "different Pueblos had their fancies in blankets. Among these must not be overlooked the white cotton wedding blanket of the Hopi, ceremonially woven by the groom for his bride, afterward embroidered with symbolic designs, and at death wrapped around her body in preparation for the last rites. In the same tribe much embroidered cotton blankets are worn by women impersonators in several ceremonies, also a small shoulder blanket in white, dark blue, and red, forming part of woman's 'full dress' as well as a ceremonial garment."[4]

Shields also explains that, "after the advent of the whites, the blankets leaped into sudden prominence with tribes that had no weaving and had previously worn robes, the preparation of which was most exhausting."[5] Whether

it was of native- or machine-made origin, the American Indian's robe is described as a practical accouterment in most early accounts from every region of the continent.

As for the blanket's functionality, Navajo weaving historian Charles Avery Amsden wrote, "In this useful garment, worn over the shoulders and frequently belted at the waist, the wearer could muffle his head against the cold or shield his face from the sun or the driving sand of desert windstorms. Burdens of every description, from firewood to babies, were carried in its folds. Like the Arab's *burnous*, it was a garment by day, a blanket by night, an inseparable companion in all seasons. Today, the machine-made blankets and shawls known as 'Pendletons' have replaced it; but its form and proportion survive still."[6]

The 1890 *Report on Indians Taxed and*
Not Taxed describes groups of Indian people gathering daily near the Tusayan Trading Post owned by Thomas V. Keams in the canyon that bears his name. The government agent writes, "I must mention the blankets, which are of various designs and colors... they form not only an indispensable part of the Indians' wardrobe, but also serve as their bed covering at night or day, whatever time they take for sleep. The blanket is generally wrapped about one its full length, covering the head and falling below the knees, and is girdled about the waist by a cartridge belt, or by the more ornamental and expensive belt made by the Navajo silversmith. When not used for shoulder or head covering, the upper part is allowed to fall and form a double skirt, which falls gracefully about the legs."

But we now know the robe is imbued with more than just practical

significance; it has become a standard of exchange, a measure of wealth and standing, even a medium to express emotion and meaning. While superficial observation might see the robe as a simple garment, it has been an integral part of the dynamic Native American life and culture for centuries. As Luther Standing Bear explains in his autobiography, the robe is "worn with the significance of language."

As Patrick Houlihan points out, the twenty-seventh annual report of the Bureau of American Ethnology (BAE), published in 1905, includes an extensive explanation of "the language of the robe" (see pictures on pages vi through ix). This account explains that "while each man wore his robe in a manner characteristic of the individual, either gracefully or otherwise, yet there was a typical way of expressing certain purposes or feelings by the adjustment of the robe that was persistent and easily recognizeable." The report goes on to explain the specific ways in which both men and women gathered the robe about them or draped it over their shoulders to convey emotions and moods. One example depicts "a young man walking. The robe is thrown loosely over the left shoulder and gathered on the left arm. The right arm is free and the limbs unencumbered. The folds of the garment add grace and dignity to the figure."

Again, note that a blanket was used in the BAE photographs instead of a buffalo robe. This was no doubt for convenience at the time, but it also points out how completely the blanket replaced the robe made from hide among the Plains tribes. In fact, trade blankets were, and are, often referred to as "robes."

An example of this use of the blanket is in the photograph made in about 1930 of Patricio Calabaza and Rafael Lobato, two men from Santo Domingo Pueblo. The man on the left is carrying a striped Navajo-woven blanket; the man on the right is carrying a Pendleton trade blanket. Both men have the precisely folded blanket draped over the left shoulder just as described in the BAE report, making the patterns and textures a striking part of their individual identities. This is another example of how the commercially produced trade blanket replaced the hand-woven textiles among the Native American people. Because the trade blanket was a finer weave, it was softer and easier to use as a wearing blanket—and, of course, often more readily available than the hand-woven Navajo or Pueblo textiles.

Another use of the robe, the Bureau of Ethnology report explains, depicts the pose of the man who stands watching some transaction of public interest. His attitude is quiet and firm, the robe is definitely adjusted,...but there is no indecision in the mind of the wearer—he will be ready for speech or act when the opportune moment arrives.

Perhaps the most striking illustration of this expressive use of the garment was its adjustment in the case of anger. Stung by sudden wrong or injury, the man grasps the edges of his robe and hastily draws it up

DR. WHIRLWIND. NOTE HOW THE BLANKET BECOMES A PART OF HIS "DRESSED" ATTIRE. (PHOTO BY MAJOR LEE MOORHOUSE, COURTESY UNIVERSITY OF OREGON LIBRARY)

over his head, thus withdrawing from observation.

Another photograph that depicts the use of the blanket as an expressive part of both an individual's personality and a collective native identity is the image titled "Blackfeet Warriors Ready for Sun Dance." Each of the five men holds his blanket folded over his arm. Even in such carefully posed photographs, the blanket is clearly as much a part of the individual's identity as the headdress.

The Moorhouse photograph of Dr. Whirlwind, Cayuse tribe, shows a different way to wear the blanket—folded and wrapped around the waist, with the patterns of the blanket merging on

either side of the fold. Dr. Whirlwind, his blanket an important part of his imposing presence, is standing against a photographer's backdrop with his lever-action rifle, the stock of which is decorated with brass studs in cross-pattern elements.

Commerce or trade in blankets woven by native weavers was established long before the advent of the commercially woven trade blanket. Just as the trade blanket replaced hide robes among Plains tribes, it replaced hand-loomed blankets in the Southwest—both for trade and for practical use. First, there was the introduction of European- and English-made blankets for use in the fur trade during the mid-seventeenth century.

In relatively recent times, Navajo-made blankets were traded among Indian and white people up and down the Great Plains.

With the opening of the Santa Fe Trail in 1822 and the ensuing greatly expanded eastern trade with the Southwest, Navajo weaving becomes common enough to study. In what is generally known as the classic period—prior to 1880—we find that the textiles were all blankets, used as saddle blankets, or worn as dresses by the women and as outer garments by both sexes of all ages. So finely woven were these blankets that they became a valuable trade item with other tribes, sometimes reaching groups as far away from Navajo country as the Sioux of the Dakotas. Soldiers and ranchers prized these textiles as warm and watertight bedding. Indeed, in 1850 a Navajo blanket was so highly valued that it was priced at fifty dollars in gold, a very considerable sum at that time.[7]

Illustrating this well-documented

trade in blankets is the photograph of the Jicarilla Apache couple at Taos. Taos has been an important Southwestern trade center for generations—an important point where Puebloan and Plains cultures met and later where fur traders and trappers conducted business. Perhaps this couple was visiting Taos to share in the dances as well as exchange trade goods. This photograph shows different but typical styles of wearing the blanket. Another image which confirms the importance of trade blankets is the photograph of the San Juan man, perhaps visiting for the Comanche dances. In addition to his blanket, he's wearing Plains leggings decorated with beaded strips.

Here the question "What is an Indian blanket?" arises. The Navajo classic blanket is certainly an "Indian blanket" because it was woven by Indian artisans and used by Indian people. The trade blankets—from the earliest Hudson's Bay blanket to the contemporary Pendleton—was a blanket designed and manufactured for the Indian trade. In common usage, it is just as much an "Indian blanket" because it has been defined in terms of the native cultures.

Nineteenth-century ledger drawings depict Indians of different Plains tribes wearing striped Navajo blankets and *kapotes*, a type of heavy overcoat fashioned from commercially manufactured Hudson's Bay blankets. Ledger drawings of the period include Plains people wearing both Navajo-woven striped blankets and trade blankets. Gradually, trade blankets completely replaced the native textiles.

In his two-volume history of the

JOHN CONCHA AND DAUGHTER ISABEL, TAOS PUEBLO, C. 1920. THEY DEMONSTRATE TWO DIFFERENT STYLES OF WEARING A BLANKET—ONE A WOMAN'S AND THE OTHER A MAN'S. (PHOTO COURTESY DENVER PUBLIC LIBRARY, WESTERN HISTORY DEPARTMENT)

Cheyenne, *People of the Sacred Mountain*, Father Peter Powell relates an account of the importance of the trade blanket in courting found in the Little Wolf ledger:

About the time of the wars with the veʔhoʔe, the young men of the People adopted the old-fashioned Lakota form of courting. When a young man became fond of a young woman, he went close to the lodge in which she lived, wrapped in his robe or blanket, so that his head and face were covered. There he stood, waiting for her to come out on some errand. When she passed on her way to get water or gather wood, or on her return, he stepped up beside her and threw his arms and his blanket around her, covering her with his blanket. Holding her fast he began to talk to her, hoping that she would listen to him. If the young woman did not like this she showed it by breaking away at once, then the young man went away embarrassed. However, if she was willing to listen to him, he might talk to her at length, for an hour or two or even longer.[8]

decorate clothing, moccasins, bags, robes, and other personal items. When multicolored cut-glass beads became available through European traders, they were incorporated into designs on a similar type of loom and became a new part of the material culture of the tribes. Because they were "recast by Native American users," glass beads could be appreciated in a new context and became identified with the Native American cultures in a completely different way than they were identified with the European culture from which they originated. Because the American Indian people placed them in a completely new context, trade blankets became identified in a new way. Just as the unique designs on a beaded bag or garment expressed the tribal and individual identity of the owner, the wearing robe or trade blanket itself was a statement of "Indianness."

As the commercial market for trade blankets became more sophisticated, individual companies chose specific designs and color combinations for specific regions of the country. Because American Indian people adopted the trade blanket and used it universally, the trade blanket became more clearly a definitive statement of native identity.

In the photograph of John Concha and his daughter Isabel, we see two distinct ways of displaying the trade blanket. The man, more confident and secure in his identity, drapes the blanket over his shoulders. He is holding a beaded pipe bag, another item that might have been given to him by someone from a different tribe or for which he might have traded. Like the bag, the trade blanket is now a part of his identity.

This account of how the blanket was used during courtship is just one example of how the trade blanket became an integral part of American native lifeways. Even as the European invasion spread across the western half of North America and exerted dominance during the nineteenth century, the Indian people continued to wear the trade blanket or robe as a statement of individual and tribal identity.

Trade blankets gained a new identity in the Native American cultures in the same way commercially manufactured cut-glass beads did. Trade blankets took the place of fur and hide robes just as manufactured, cut-glass beads took the place of porcupine quills in geometric and floral loomed or applique designs.

For generations, quills had been dyed, split, and woven into unique designs specific to tribes and individuals. This quillwork was then used to

Isabel Concha, unlike her father, reveals her shyness with the way she has wrapped the blanket over her head and is clutching it beneath her chin. She is almost hidden from view; only her face and her eyes, watching the outside world, are visible. In this photograph, the way father and daughter use the trade blanket reveals something very distinctive about the individual.

Even if draped or tied over a standard white man's suit, as one of the old men has done for the photograph of the two against a canyon wall, the trade blanket made a strong statement about the wearer. Each man has adopted a different means of displaying the blanket, and each has made it uniquely his own. It is clear that each man *chose* to add the trade blanket to his person in order to make a statement about his personal identity. The blankets are not required in place of other garments but are a preferred garment.

And the language of the robe was widely understood among both men and women of many tribes. The photograph titled "Four Young Indian Women" captures each woman wearing the trade blanket or fringed shawl draped over the shoulders in a similar way—natural, comfortable and at ease. In contrast, in the photograph of the Pueblo woman in the banded blanket, we see someone who is more shy, using the blanket as a shield to hide the mystery of her identity.

In these historic photographs, it is clear that the blanket is an important

part of the American Indian identity. In fact, the term "blanket Indian" was used by non-Indians to refer to the traditional people that kept to the old ways, as opposed to those of the native population that more readily adopted the white styles of dress and abandoned their trade blankets. Even though "blanket Indian" seems to have a pejorative connotation in the context of the white culture, it still points out how completely the trade blanket or wearing robe came to symbolize North America's native cultures. The two elderly men in the photograph are certainly "blanket Indians," and the use of the blanket is a sign of each person's individuality and even of his creativity, as well as his group identity.

However, even if we today choose

to consider the term "blanket Indian" a positive one, it is probable that, when the United States' 1890 census used the term to describe the traditionals among the native population, it had more negative connotations. "Blanket Indian" became an institutionalized term. It was no doubt applied hurriedly and without thought for the complex meanings that would be attached to the trade blanket as symbol. Even so, it does acknowledge the trade blanket as a symbol that immediately categorizes the traditional people and identifies an entire way of life.[9]

For generations, individual Indian people have chosen the blanket to make a statement of everyday belonging to the Indian community. In the course of a Pueblo feast day, a woman might be in the house cooking, wearing a cotton print dress. But before she goes out to join the group dancing in the plaza of the pueblo, she wraps herself in a fringed shawl—a symbol of her belonging to the community. At the moment she wraps herself in the shawl, she is transformed. She's wrapped in a different identity.

This statement is confirmed in the photograph of the Ute Bear Dance, in which we see a line of people taking part in the ceremony—all wrapped in blankets. The individuals in the group create a magic poetic movement, a harmonious and rhythmic motion that is not only hypnotically beautiful but also expresses their unity. The same is true of the group of Pueblo men in the photograph on page 16, some drumming, but all unified visually. And the trade blanket is a part of that unified statement.

And even though the trade blanket

is more often associated with the Pueblo and Plains people, the Asahel Curtis photograph of Chief Joseph John posed in ceremonial clothing at Tofino, Vancouver Island, shows that the trade blanket was adopted into the Northwest Coast tribes as well. In this case, the trade blanket is embellished with feathers and worn along with the elaborately carved wooden

CHIEF JOSEPH JOHN, TOFINO, VANCOUVER ISLAND, C. 1931. THE FEATHERS ATTACHED TO THIS TRADE BLANKET HAVE TRANSFORMED IT INTO A CEREMONIAL ROBE. (PHOTO BY ASAHEL CURTIS, COURTESY WASHINGTON STATE HISTORICAL SOCIETY, TACOMA)

mask to become part of the individual's ceremonial identity.

To make this statement of identity even more clear—to make the language of the robe even more eloquent—each tribe enhanced the trade blanket in its own distinctive designs. The people of several Plains tribes sewed beaded blanket strips onto the trade blankets, enhancing both the blanket's value and

INDIAN WOMAN
CARRYING HER CHILD
IN A FOLD OF THE
BLANKET. (PHOTO
COURTESY WESTERN
HISTORY COLLECTIONS,
UNIVERSITY OF
OKLAHOMA LIBRARY)

INDIAN WOMAN CARRYING HER CHILD IN A FOLD OF THE BLANKET. (PHOTO COURTESY WESTERN HISTORY COLLECTIONS, UNIVERSITY OF OKLAHOMA LIBRARY)

its visual appeal, and the Prairie Sac and Fox made their blankets distinctive with appliqué and embroidery.

Traditionally, the trade blanket has been a part of the Native American's earliest memories. As Rain Parrish relates in her essay in Chapter One, during infancy, children are wrapped in soft, warm trade blankets. As they grow older, blankets are gifts which commemorate important milestones and achievements. Throughout life, trade blankets are a measure of individual identity and continue as a standard of exchange. And, at death, each person is wrapped in a favorite blanket for the transition to the next world. In the photograph of the men and women mourning a lost relative, we can feel the emotion in the hearts of the people.

By studying the language of the robe, the language of the American Indian trade blanket, we can understand the power of a culture recasting an object in a new way. This language explains a living tradition among the Native American people. Within the tribe or pueblo, the blanket is a state-

KOOTENAI INDIAN WOMAN IS USING A BLANKET AS A SADDLE BLANKET. SMALL CHILD ON THE TRAVOIS BEHIND THE HORSE IS ALSO WRAPPED IN A BLANKET. (PHOTO COURTESY OREGON HISTORICAL SOCIETY)

ment of an individual's bond to the older, traditional ways, to roots that run deep. It's also a statement of personal identity. The blanket continues as a standard of exchange; and as a gift, the blanket is an important acknowledgement of friendship, gratitude, and respect. The language of the robe is a language that allows an eloquence unknown to the spoken word.

THREE NAVAJO WEAVERS C. 1910. WHILE CREATING WEAVINGS FOR THE NON-INDIAN MARKET, THESE WOMEN KEEP WARM BY WEARING AND SITTING ON COMMERCIALLY WOVEN TRADE BLANKETS. (PHOTO BY WILL PENNINGTON, COURTESY BOB KAPOUN)

THE CUSTOM OF BURYING PEOPLE IN THEIR FAVORITE BLANKETS IS STILL PRACTICED AMONG NATIVE AMERICAN PEOPLE. (PHOTO COURTESY OREGON HISTORICAL SOCIETY)

DELEGATION OF PAWNEE LEADERS, WASHINGTON, D.C.,
C. 1875. NOTE HOW EACH MAN IS WEARING HIS HUDSON'S BAY
BLANKET IN A DIFFERENT STYLE. (PHOTO BY C. M. BELL,
COURTESY F. H. DOUGLAS LIBRARY, DENVER ART MUSEUM)

SECTION TWO
A HISTORY OF THE BLANKET

THE BLANKET IN THE FUR TRADE

BEGINNING IN THE EARLIEST YEARS OF THE DUTCH EAST INDIA COMPANY'S FORAYS INTO THE NEW WORLD, THE NORTH AMERICAN FUR TRADE WAS PRIMARILY A MEANS OF EXPLOITING THE UNEXPLORED CONTINENT'S NATURAL WEALTH. IN THE EARLY- TO MID-SEVENTEENTH CENTURY, THE DUTCH TRADE IN THE AMERICAS WAS HEADQUARTERED IN NEW AMSTERDAM. DURING THIS PERIOD, A SUCCESSFUL FRENCH FUR TRADE WAS ESTABLISHED IN THE SAINT LAWRENCE RIVER VALLEY. AT THE SAME TIME, THE ENGLISH HUDSON'S BAY COMPANY ALSO MADE ITS PRESENCE KNOWN IN CANADA. • HUDSON'S BAY COMPANY ESTABLISHED ITS OPERATIONS ALONG THE SOUTHERN REACHES OF HUDSON BAY BY THE MID-1600S. IN ORDER TO TAKE PART IN THE HUDSON'S BAY COMMERCE, NATIVES MADE THE JOURNEY FROM THEIR HOME COUNTRY IN THE NORTHERN WOODLANDS TO THE TRADING POSTS ON HUDSON BAY ALONG INLAND WATERWAYS, OFTEN AS MUCH AS FIVE HUNDRED MILES, WITH HEAVILY LOADED CANOES, FOR THE TRADING SEASON. FOLLOWING THE EXCHANGE OF FURS FOR GUNS, BLANKETS, TOBACCO, AND BRANDY, THEY RETURNED HOME WITH THE TRADE GOODS THAT WOULD CHANGE THEIR LIVES AND CULTURES IRREVERSIBLY. THE CONTACT AND TRADE REPRESENTED A SIGNIFICANT CHANGE IN THE NATIVE WAY OF LIFE, AND THE INTRODUCTION OF THE TRADE BLANKET WAS ONE OF THE MOST SIGNIFICANT. THIS WAS THE BEGINNING OF THE "reinvention" of the trade blanket within the context of American Indian cultures.

In the Northeast and the Hudson Bay region, the Indian people were cultivated as contacts and, initially, Europeans and Englishmen made little effort to learn about the country beyond the immediate coastal region that supplied lumber for construction and game for food. There was little concern for gaining an understanding of the native people except as a means to the furs, and in almost every case where an individual or group made an effort to know and understand the natives, the ulterior motive was to enhance the fur trade.

The early years of the fur trade defined a period dominated by freewheeling risk-takers. As the trade evolved and became established and more competitive, some individuals made the demanding and dangerous effort to travel inland, learning the lay of the land as well as the customs and languages of the native people. Each explorer was required to keep a journal for his employer's records, and some of these journal entries indicate a respect—even an affection or admiration—for the native people. But beyond the anecdotes documented in these individual journal entries, there was no understanding about the blankets and uses made for them. While there are no written records that explain the significance of the wearing robe or the potential adoption of trade blankets by Indian people to replace other types of robes, there are visual records of the use of Hudson's Bay blankets in nineteenth-century photographs and Plains ledger drawings.

In one drawing from the Yellow

HUDSON'S BAY BLANKETS STACKED FOR THE POTLATCH (GIVEAWAY) CEREMONY, KWAKIUTL, FORT RUPERT, BRITISH COLUMBIA. (PHOTO COURTESY F. H. DOUGLAS LIBRARY, DENVER ART MUSEUM)

Horse Ledger titled "A Warbonnet Man Fights a Crow," the artist depicts a mounted Crow warrior wearing a Hudson's Bay kapote with the characteristic green, red, black and yellow stripes.[1]

In the photograph of Hudson's Bay blankets for a potlatch, we can appreciate the value of the trade blankets among the tribes of the Northwest Coast region, where this photograph was made. The person holding the potlatch has assembled more than five hundred blankets to give away in the course of the event, an astounding statement of the importance of the trade blanket as a medium of exchange. This photograph shows how the trade blanket had replaced other types of goods used in the potlatch or Give-away in the Northwest. By 1992 standards, that collection of blankets is probably worth at least $50,000.

As the fur trade expanded in the southwestern and western regions of what is now the United States, the early trappers and mountain men made contact with the tribes and came to know the Indian people well, in some cases living with people for extended periods and even marrying into the tribes. Many accounts of the period's fur trade relate romantic stories of a peaceful coexistence between Indian people and the early trappers. But if it truly existed, this peaceful coexistence was short-lived. After the fur trade became organized to maximize profits, trapping operations became less willing to acknowledge the native people because they generally hindered trapping operations and so stood in the way of efficiently taking the maximum

number of furs. Once the larger organizations took over the fur trade, it was no longer characterized by the individual bartering for pelts but was an industry looking to increase profits for investors in the eastern states. The occasional tribute was paid to a tribe for the right to trap on its land, and some commercial interaction was necessary. But agents for the major trading companies generally considered the

SAC AND FOX MAN C. 1868, WEARING A HUDSON'S BAY BLANKET EMBELLISHED WITH RIBBON APPLIQUÉ. THE APPLIQUÉ DESIGNS ARE THE FLORAL PATTERNS MORE TYPICAL OF THE WOODLANDS TRIBES. (PHOTO COURTESY THE THOMAS GILCREASE INSTITUTE OF AMERICAN HISTORY AND ART, TULSA, OK)

Indians to be an inconvenience. And, unfortunately, the most commonly expressed sentiment among the Europeans and naturalized Americans was the attitude of the Hudson's Bay Company traders in the late seventeenth century that

the Indians were savages to be traded with and distrusted; and the interior was full of

UTE MAN C. 1880S, WEARING A HUDSON'S BAY BLANKET WITH A BEADED BLANKET STRIP SEWN ONTO IT. THE BEADWORK ENHANCES THE BLANKET'S VALUE AND VISUAL APPEAL. (PHOTO BY ULKE, COURTESY DEVER PUBLIC LIBRARY, WESTERN HISTORY DEPARTMENT)

unknown terrors... Furthermore, the Englishmen, engaged by the season, had no consuming desire to become intimate with the ways of the forest...[2]

With the handsome returns on investment in the fur trade, a little trust certainly went a long way. The trade with the natives was lucrative. Historian Douglas Mackay writes about one early voyage to Hudson Bay:

It is known that tools and trinkets for the Indian trade were valued at six hundred and fifty pounds, and the *Nonsuch* on her return voyage brought to London on October 9, 1669, furs worth nineteen thousand pounds. The glowing, expansive language of the Royal Charter reflected the percentage of return. Here truly must be an empire overseas, with profits for those who came early.[3]

In the mid-nineteenth century, historian Hubert Howe Bancroft reports that a trader could use English or European trinkets valued at about a dollar to purchase furs in the Northwest Coast region. These furs could be sold in China and the profits invested in tea, silk or other Asian goods that could be shipped back to New York and sold for twenty dollars or more.[4]

There was little concern among the Europeans to learn why the native people chose to use trade blankets. So long as they were happy with the guns, brandy, blankets, or trade trinkets, there was little reason to question the importance of the trade blankets themselves.

Even though few people of the time commented on the cultural importance of the trade blanket, its commercial importance was never questioned. In fact, the blanket itself became acknowledged as a standard of trade. The traders developed a system to regulate the fur trade. First, the beaver

SHOSHONE FAMILY C. 1870S. THE WOMAN SEATED ON LEFT IS WEARING A NAVAJO CHIEF'S STYLE BLANKET. THE MAN STANDING IS WEARING A STRIPED HUDSON'S BAY CHIEF'S STYLE BLANKET. (PHOTO COURTESY F. H. DOUGLAS LIBRARY, DENVER ART MUSEUM)

UTE MAN C. 1915, WITH HUDSON'S BAY BLANKET DRAPED OVER HIS HORSE. NOTE THE THREE THIN STRIPES THAT INDICATE THE BLANKET'S WEIGHT IN POINTS. (PHOTO BY H. F. ROBINSON, COURTESY MUSEUM OF NEW MEXICO, NEG. 21556)

each...and so on through a long list of trade items. These values were applicable to trade at Albany Fort, Moose River, and East Main.[5]

Of course, the value of goods traded for a beaver skin varied with the location of the fort and also changed with time.

A hundred years later, at Fort MacPherson, we find a blanket worth ten beaver-skins; a gun, twenty; a worsted belt, two; eighteen bullets, one beaver skin. The gun cost twenty-two shillings, and in London, the twenty beaver skins were then worth 32 pounds 10s.[6]

During these times, trade blankets were considered prized enough to become a standard of value. It might seem that the fur trade and other early commerce with the Native American people was rather informal. In reality, it was controlled by specific guidelines. The European trade items were divided into three classes. Tobacco, knives, and other inexpensive gifts were placed into the first class to be used by the trading companies as gifts to Indian clients. These small, inexpensive gifts were simply "giveaways" and would usually attract customers and bring the giver enhanced trading status.

The next class of trade goods included ammunition, blankets, guns, and anything else that was used only for barter or direct trade for furs. These were the most important and most valuable trade goods. The third class included all the "odds and ends"—handkerchiefs, beads, and any other type of good that was traded for game or given in exchange for services.

Another formalized or standardized aspect of the fur trade that is particularly important to the history of the trade blanket is the point system for grading

skin became the standard and the values of all other furs, skins, and European or English trade items were measured by "the beaver-skin standard." In 1733, Bancroft writes that

with the skin of one full-grown beaver, a native could buy a half a pound of beads, or one pound of Brazil tobacco, or half a pound of thread. A gallon of brandy cost four beaver-skins, broadcloth, two beaver-skins a year, and blankets, six beaver skins

furs. The "point" became a unit of trade, equivalent to a currency standard. One point equaled one good, full-size beaver skin. The value of any trade item, previously stated in numbers of skins—the beaver standard—was eventually stated in points. By this point system, a trade blanket valued at three points was worth three good, full-size beaver skins. The point system was expanded to include all trade items and all kinds of skins or furs. The number of points referred to the weight of the blankets themselves.

The evolution of the point system is another example of how the fur trade

became more sophisticated and, as a further indication of the importance of the trade blanket in this system, the blanket was adopted as a medium of exchange with a very specific value. Each type of blanket was given a certain number of points according to its weight and it was referred to as a three-and-a-half-point blanket, or a two-point blanket and so forth. What had originally referred to the number of beaver or other skins the company had taken in trade now also referred to the weight of a trade blanket. Each trade blanket was given a stripe for each point and a half-stripe for each half-

A PAIR OF HUDSON'S BAY THREE-POINT BLANKETS. THE BLANKETS WERE SHIPPED TO NORTH AMERICA FROM ENGLAND AS PAIRS. THEY COULD BE CUT DOWN THE CENTER TO MAKE TWO BLANKETS, OR LEFT LIKE THIS AND USED FOR BOTH A BOTTOM AND TOP BLANKET

HUDSON'S BAY CHIEF
BLANKET. THIS STYLE IS
PRODUCED TODAY
WITH THE BANDS IN
THE SAME FOUR
COLORS AS IN EARLY
YEARS: BLACK,
YELLOW, RED, AND
GREEN ON WHITE
BACKGROUND.

point to indicate its weight. A three-point blanket had three small stripes woven into one border to give the customer an inde-pendent measure of its weight. The points still signified the price of the blanket in "made beaver" and each unit represented one good, full-size beaver skin.

According to records of the Hudson's Bay Co-mpany, the earliest reference to any commercial blankets being used for trade is from 1682. The first specific mention of the famous, specially designed Hudson's Bay blanket was made in 1740. A Hudson's Bay

blanket was heavy, since it was pure wool—both warp and weft. It was significantly heavier than the contemporary trade blankets, that almost always had a cotton warp. The blankets traded between 1682 and 1740 were probably commercial English blankets that did not carry the Hudson's Bay Company label. But, at any rate, the blankets became a staple trade item soon after they were introduced. The Hudson's Bay blankets were woven in England, initially in the factory owned by the Empson family of Witney. The Empson family maintained the trade with the Hudson's Bay Company through at least 1785, and the first records of other companies supplying the Hudson's Bay Company are dated 1805.

Witney was a commercial weaving center that was home to upwards of thirty blanket manufacturers in the early years of the nineteenth century. By 1832, the number of mills had dwindled to only five. And, according to one order book covering the years 1823 to 1828, about one-half the orders were for export, many of these blankets intended for the North American fur trade. One order dated January 1824 was for 7,539 pairs of Point blankets. Another order for Point blankets asked that the blankets 'be packed in Small Bales being for the Indian Trade.' The reference is to the North American Indians, and the bales had to be small so as to load easily into canoes to travel the Canadian rivers.[7]

Blankets were certainly used as an item of trade as soon as the Europeans began to trade blankets for furs to the tribes of the Northern Plains. As the

CROW CHIEFS, MONTANA, 1887. BESIDES BEING WRAPPED IN BLANKETS, SEVERAL MEN ARE WEARING KAPOTES, COATS MADE FROM TRADE BLANKETS. (PHOTO COURTESY WESTERN HISTORY COLLECTIONS, UNIVERSITY OF OKLAHOMA LIBRARY)

ledger drawings indicate, the Hudson's Bay blankets made their way onto the Plains and were prized possessions.

As trade evolved, the blanket was no longer simply a sought-after commodity; it was a standard of exchange in itself. Even though it was not as completely standardized and as well documented as the point system in the Hudson's Bay fur trade, the blanket trade in the Southwest and West itself was definitely an independent standard by which trade could be organized and wealth could be measured.

CHIEF JOSEPH WEARING AN EARLY PENDLETON BLANKET, 1901.
(PHOTO BY MAJOR LEE MOORHOUSE, COURTESY BOB KAPOUN)

THE ANNUITY PERIOD AND THE TRANSITION TO THE RESERVATION

BY CHARLES J. LOHRMANN

"IT IS COLD AND WE HAVE NO BLANKETS. THE LITTLE CHILDREN ARE FREEZING TO DEATH. MY
PEOPLE, SOME OF THEM, HAVE RUN AWAY TO THE HILLS AND HAVE NO BLANKETS, NO FOOD. NO
ONE KNOWS WHERE THEY ARE—PERHAPS FREEZING TO DEATH. I WANT TO HAVE TIME TO LOOK
FOR MY CHILDREN AND SEE HOW MANY OF THEM I CAN FIND. MAYBE I SHALL FIND THEM
AMONG THE DEAD. HEAR ME, MY CHIEFS. I AM TIRED; MY HEART IS SICK AND SAD. FROM WHERE
THE SUN NOW STANDS, I WILL FIGHT NO MORE FOREVER."

....

CHIEF JOSEPH

CHIEF JOSEPH'S POIGNANT STATEMENT CHARACTERIZES THE PERIOD THAT MARKED THE TRANSITION THE AMERICAN INDIAN PEOPLE WERE FORCED TO MAKE WHEN THEIR FREEDOM HAD BEEN COMPLETELY DESTROYED. DURING THE END OF THE NINETEENTH CENTURY, THE LAST FREE-MOVING GROUPS WERE TRACKED DOWN, SUBDUED BY FORCE, AND MOVED ONTO RESERVATIONS. THIS SUBJUGATION PROCESS WAS THE CULMINATION OF A CENTURY OF DIFFICULT AND LARGELY UNSUCCESSFUL NEGOTIATIONS WITH THE UNITED STATES GOVERNMENT. AND THE CENTURY ENDED WITH STATEMENTS LIKE CHIEF JOSEPH'S AND WITH NATIVE AMERICAN UPRISINGS AND IMPRISIONMENTS. • THE NEGOTIATING BETWEEN THE AMERICAN INDIAN PEOPLE AND THE UNITED STATES GOVERNMENT BEGAN IN 1776, WHEN THE NEWLY FORMED FEDERAL GOVERNMENT UNDERTOOK NEGOTIATION OF TREATIES REGARDING LAND AND MUTUAL DEFENSE ISSUES WITH THE INDIVIDUAL TRIBES. IN ADDITION TO THE AGREEMENTS REGARDING RIGHTS TO LANDS, THESE TREATIES ALMOST ALWAYS REQUIRED PAYMENT OF TRADE GOODS TO THE INDIAN PEOPLE BY THE UNITED STATES GOVERNMENT. AN 1890 CENSUS BUREAU REPORT ON INDIANS TAXED AND NOT TAXED CASTS SOME LIGHT ON THE TANGLED HISTORY OF THE UNITED STATES GOVERNMENT'S INDIAN POLICY. THIS 1890 REPORT EXPLAINS THAT, BEFORE THE CURRENT CONSTITUTION WAS ADOPTED, THE

United States government's Indian affairs were handled according to the Articles of Confederation. In June 1784 the Secretary in the war office was directed to order a force of militia to be raised for the purpose, to be marched to the places the commissioners for negotiating treaties with the Indians should direct.

Two months later, in August 1784, an ordinance for the regulation of Indian affairs was adopted. "All business with the Indians was to be transacted at an outpost occupied by troops of the United States." After the creation of the War Department in 1789, Indian affairs were left under the charge of the Secretary of War.

The annuities that were to be paid to the Indian tribes as a part of treaty obligations were paid by army officers who were agents of the United States War Department. Eventually, as the Indian people were confined to reservations west of the Mississippi, the Indian trade became an important and well-established business. Agencies were required to fulfill the government obligations, and government contracts were lucrative for the traders who were commissioned to manage the agencies. In the photograph taken April 17, 1882, at Fort Randall, North Dakota, United States Army officers are delivering large bales of annuity blankets that have been transported in suitcase-like containers.

Indian policy was affected by the

ISSUING OF ANNUITY GOODS AT FORT RANDALL, APIRL 17, 1882, BY POST QUARTERMASTER. (PHOTO BY STANLEY J. MORROW, COURTESY F. H. DOUGLAS LIBRARY, DENVER ART MUSEUM)

political maneuvering that resulted in the eventual transition of the Indian office from the military to civil control. When the Department of Indian Affairs was organized in 1834, it remained primarily under the jurisdiction of the War Department. The Indian office was a bureau of the War Department, but the commissioner of the office was under the control of the secretary of war and the president. No doubt the president wanted the power to keep an active hand in regulating Indian affairs because this was such a dangerous and politically sensitive topic. Virtually every citizen, every public official, and every special-interest group had a well-formed opinion about Indian policy and did not hesitate to voice it.

While the political wrangling continued in Washington and eastern cities, white settlers were continuing to encroach on Indian lands in the West, and the government officials recognized the political importance of maintaining the power to use the militia in dealing with the resulting conflict. Following the mid-century war with Mexico, the Bureau of Indian Affairs was transferred to the Department of Interior, and policies affecting native people finally came from civil rather than military officials.

Just as important as the political storms around the government's Indian policy was the United States government's official policy on trade with the Indians—known as the factor system—which was initiated in 1786. The basic principle of this system was that the government would supply the physical wants of the Indian people with commodities and annuities but would not make a profit on this commerce. Trade stations, or factories, were established along the frontier and the Indian agent, or factor, was stationed at one of these trading posts along with a clerk and an interpreter. The factor would provide goods of all kinds to the Indian people and would receive furs or pelts in exchange. These agencies were required to provide commodities (food and rations) and annuities (material goods, including blankets).

In 1810, the chairman of the Senate Committee on Indian Affairs published a list of the fourteen trade houses that had been established across the country between 1795 and 1808. This was the beginning of the policy of Manifest Destiny, a time that was romanticized and distorted with tall tales about the mountain men and the frontiersmen. It was the beginning of seemingly endless efforts to "civilize" the American Indian people.

Officially, the factor system was an attempt to maintain some control of the Indian trade and keep it from becoming completely corrupted. But in spite of any good intentions, there were charges of corruption from the beginning. And there was pressure from private citizens who saw the opportunity for tremendous profit in the fur trade. By 1822 private trading companies, including the Missouri Fur Company and John Jacob Astor's American Fur Company, became powerful enough to supplant the government trade organization.

Between 1822 and 1849, the Indian people were under the jurisdiction of the War Department. After the Interior Department was organized in 1849, a

CROW INDIANS, WASHINGTON, D.C., 1873. THE TWO MEN ON THE LEFT ARE WEARING HUDSON'S BAY BLANKETS. THE THIRD IS WEARING A SMALL BANDED ANNUITY BLANKET, MANUFACTURER UNKNOWN. (PHOTO BY ULKE, COURTESY MUSEUM OF NEW MEXICO, NEG. 58641)

system of superintendencies in each state or territory was developed. Under this system, each state's superintendent was appointed by the president to manage Indian affairs, including trade, within the state. In each territory, the territorial governor was often the superintendent. This system provided ample opportunity for corruption of the Indian trade and it was abolished in 1869, when President Ulysses Grant gave a new twist to Indian policy.

By that time, Grant, with the help of General P. H. Sheridan, decided that no more treaties should be negotiated and that the Indian people should be confined to reservations. Because the white settlers continued to illegally encroach on any Indian land that was even remotely desirable, even the restrictive reservation system was not workable. The reservation system was replaced by the allotment system through which each individual member of the tribe was allotted a parcel of land and expected to make a living from it.

Even though the official United States Indian policy changed over the decades of the nineteenth century, the necessity for trade remained constant. The market for trade blankets flourished. Indian agents and traders often enjoyed a captive market—literally, in some cases. In the Southwest, trading posts were established in Oklahoma, in New Mexico, and across the Navajo Reservation.

Trading in areas like the Navajo Reservation was more open to the market. Limited travel over rugged terrain meant that trading posts in places like Ganado became popular meeting spots for a variety of people from all walks of life. After the railroad was opened through the Southwest and across the Navajo Reservation, access to trade goods was increased dramatically. With the coming of the railroad, the traders could bring in trade blankets by the carload. More woolen manufacturers saw an opportunity to compete in the American Indian blanket trade. As competition stiffened, companies introduced more colorful trade blankets in a greater variety of colors.

In the Navajo country of the Southwest, the trade in blankets was well developed.

Until about 1875, the products of Navajo looms were blankets for their own wear and for trading to other Indians. By the 1880s stores operated by white traders sprang up in the most remote corners of

the reservation. The shelves of the trading posts offered clothing, utensil and processed food. Inexpensive, machine-made blankets from Pendleton, Oregon, appealed to women who heretofore might spend half a year weaving a blanket of similar size... Far away from the railroad, a Navajo weaver might wear a cotton skirt, velvet blouse and Pendleton blanket, but her handiwork would bring cash and credit at her trading posts.[1]

The two components of "the blanket standard" were the shawl and the robe.

Pendleton blankets came in two grades. A fringe made the difference between a shawl and a robe. It used to cost us seven dollars for a robe and eight dollars for a shawl, and I suppose Cotton made a dollar profit either way. And he sold worlds of them—the Indians wouldn't buy anything else.[2]

When C. N. Cotton established his wholesale business, C. N. Cotton Company in Gallup, New Mexico, he illustrated his astuteness by obtaining exclusive regional control of two items basic to the Navajo trade: Arbuckle's coffee and Pendleton blankets. To most Navajos of that time, any coffee or blanket under another name was either counterfeit or an inferior substitute.[3]

HUBBELL TRADING POST, GANADO, ARIZONA. PAINTING BY E. A. BURBANK, 1908. A TYPICAL SCENE AT THE TRADING POST, C. 1880S. (COURTESY U.S DEPT. OF THE INTERIOR, HUBBELL TRADING POST N.H.S., HUTR 3457)

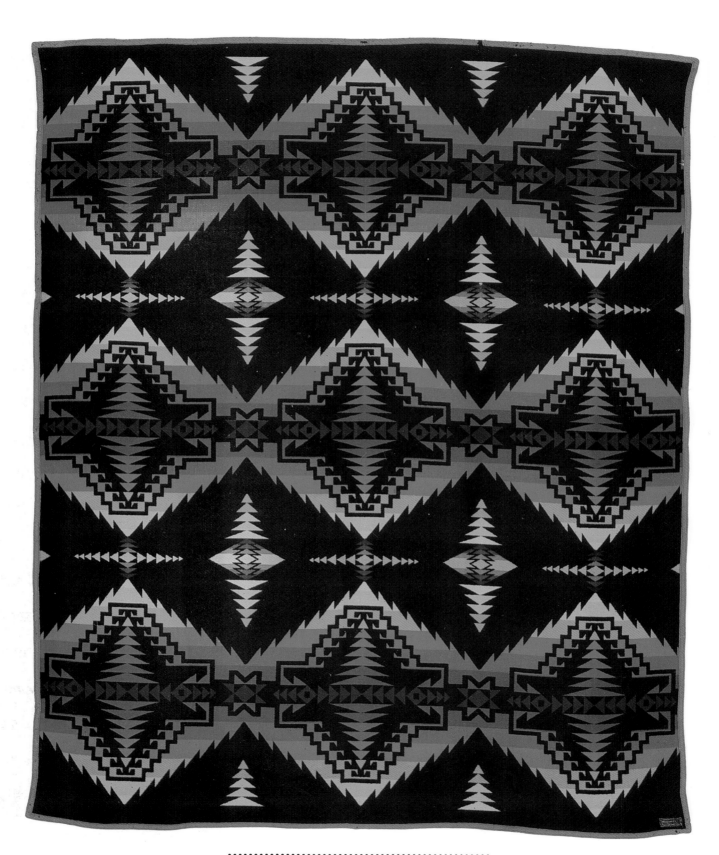

PENDLETON NINE ELEMENT ROBE, 1921 LABEL.

CHAPTER FIVE

A HISTORY OF WOOLEN MILLS
IN NORTH AMERICA

THROUGHOUT THE COLONIAL PERIOD, ENGLAND CONTROLLED THE WOOL AND WEAVING INDUSTRY IN THE AMERICAN COLONIES. INITIALLY, THE ONLY SHEEP ALLOWED IN THE COLONIES WERE THOSE BREEDS CHOSEN FOR THEIR MUTTON RATHER THAN FOR THEIR WOOL. SINCE THE FINER, LONGER WOOLS WERE NOT PRODUCED IN THE AMERICAS, SPINNING AND WEAVING WERE STRICTLY COTTAGE INDUSTRIES AND AMERICAN WOOLEN PRODUCTS, MADE FROM THE POORER WOOL, WERE COARSE AND NOT COMMERCIALLY VIABLE. • BECAUSE ENGLAND FORBADE THE MANUFACTURE OF BLANKETS IN THE COLONIES, THE EARLIEST BLANKETS USED IN THE AMERICAN INDIAN TRADE CAME FROM ENGLAND AND EUROPE. FOLLOWING THE AMERICAN REVOLUTION, THE WOOL INDUSTRY IN THE UNITED STATES FACED A ROCKY ECONOMIC ROAD. STARTING IN NEW ENGLAND, WHERE THERE WAS A COMBINATION OF SKILLED LABOR, WATER POWER, AND RAW WOOL TO MAKE THE FACTORIES ECONOMICALLY VIABLE, THE SMALL MANUFACTURING PLANTS BEGAN OPERATION IN THE EARLY NINETEENTH CENTURY. EVEN THOUGH THERE WERE HUNDREDS OF INDEPENDENT OPERATIONS, ONLY A HANDFUL OF COMPANIES DESIGNED THEIR PRODUCTS FOR THE INDIAN TRADE. • IN THE NORTHWEST, PARTICULARLY IN OREGON, THE WOOLEN INDUSTRY DIDN'T ACHIEVE THE NECESSARY COMBINATION OF RAW MATERIALS, POWER, AND SKILLED LABOR UNTIL

OREGON CITY SIX ELEMENT ROBE, PATTERNIZATION SIDE. THE BACKGROUND COLOR ON THE PATTERNIZATION SIDE ALLOWS EASIER VIEWING OF THE PATTERN.

these eleven, only one, the Buffalo Manufacturing Company, was listed specifically as a manufacturer of Indian blankets.

The future of the trade blanket as we now know it was insured with the introduction of the Jacquard adapter loom to the United States in the 1880s. The double-shuttle Jacquard loom, developed in France in the 1840s, allowed for the creation of a blanket with a positive design on one side and a negative of the same image on the reverse. This "double-faced" design is typical of most trade blankets and gives a completely different perception of the design on opposite sides. Because the introduction of the Jacquard loom made increased production of colorful trade blankets possible, this advance helped make the period from 1880 through 1930 a "golden age" of the American Indian trade blanket.

The patterns created by the Jacquard loom were controlled by specially designed cylinders called "cards." One way to understand how these cards worked is to compare them to the cylinders that control the way a player piano plays. The cards were set to create a particular design and each firm guarded its designs carefully.

The founder of the oldest of the major American Indian trade blanket manufacturing companies—Joseph Capps—started his first wool scouring operation in 1837. Even though the wool processing industry was established in New England, Capps was an early operation for the Midwest and was two decades ahead of the earliest operation in the Oregon woolen industry.

the 1850s. Ambitious industrialists faced a series of difficult challenges in establishing a woolen mill. First, they had to find an appropriate community that could afford to support the startup of a mill. Then, there was the difficulty of raising capital and arranging construction. Finally, plans had to be made for the time-consuming and expensive transportation of the weaving machinery from New England by ship.

Among the dozens of American mills listed in the 1845 "Statistics of Woollen Manufactories in the United States," there were only eleven mills listed that manufactured blankets. Of

In Oregon, it was not until 1857 that the Willamette Woolen Manufacturing Company installed machinery that had been shipped to Oregon from New England via Cape Horn. In January 1858 the mill completed its initial run of blankets, the first of which was auctioned off for $110 and bore the label "Hard Times." By 1859 "regular demand for the mill's output in mining camps and stores was augmented by orders from Edward Geary, Superintendent of Indian Affairs, who purchased blankets for his department." By mid-1860, the sales of Willamette's "Hard Times" blankets to the Indian agency were no longer made direct from the factory but through wholesalers.[1]

With the growing market for blankets among the Indian population, particularly in the southwestern territories of the United States, the five major woolen manufacturers were vying aggressively for the attention of trading post operators and other retailers catering to the Indian trade. The woolen industry had evolved by taking advantage of more sophisticated manufacturing methods, particularly with the introduction of the Jacquard loom. Although most trade blanket patterns came from American Indian design concepts, weaving historian C. A. Amsden documented the limited influence the double-sided patterns of the trade blankets had on native weavers who, after seeing the double-sided blankets, produced a double-sided twill weaving on the native vertical loom.

The five primary competitors in the blanket market were: J. Capps and Sons (started 1837), Oregon City Woolen

OREGON CITY
SIX ELEMENT ROBE,
COLORIZATION SIDE.
(REVERSE SIDE OF
BLANKET ON
FACING PAGE)

Mills (1864), Buell Manufacturing Company (1877), Racine Woolen Mills (1877), and Pendleton Woolen Mills (1896). By the turn of the twentieth century, the vast majority of the trade blanket business was divided among these five competitors. Even though it was not the first mill in the business, Pendleton became the best known and, in the public mind, the name Pendleton is synonymous with American Indian trade blankets. This is primarily because Pendleton was the only firm to focus its resources exclusively on the Indian blanket trade. The other firms manufactured a selection of woolen

BUELL BANDED "COMANCHE" PATTERN ROBE. NOTE THAT THE THUNDERBIRDS ARE BLACK ON THIS SIDE OF THE BLANKET.

specific regions. All the companies were competing for the same national market, although there was some regional specialization. For example, Capps focused its marketing energies on the Oklahoma Indian Territory rather than on the Southwest or Northwest where Pendleton and Oregon City were stronger. It's reasonable to assume that Racine and Buell were more active closer to their headquarters, among the Indian agencies of the Northern Plains. Photographs from the Northern Plains show women wearing what were, in all likelihood, Racine's fringed shawls.

Effectively reaching the Native American market required no comprehensive marketing plans or extensive display advertising but, rather, depended more on providing a well-designed and well-manufactured blanket for the Indian customers. To reach the non-Indian markets was much more difficult. Each company developed its own advertising and promotion campaigns, usually associating its blankets with romantic images of the American Indian and the American West and hoping this romanticism would attract customers.

Each manufacturer also published at least one catalog by 1910. In addition to a romanticized version of the relationship between Indian and trade blanket or wearing robe, the catalogs usually included an illustration of a parlor or "Indian room" in a house of the period. Some companies developed a fictitious spokesperson, like the Capps Cozy Corner Girl, who told a story of how important Indian blankets were to a happy life. Many advertisers of the

products in addition to Indian trade blankets. Perhaps it was the single-minded pursuit of a primary market that gave Pendleton the edge it needed to survive the hard times of the 1930s and to be the only firm among the major trade blanket manufacturers still in business in the 1990s.

Each of the firms marketed its blankets in much the same way. For the Indian trade, the companies made some effort to design blankets to fit the preferences of the individual tribes and time displayed blankets that featured a riot of colors and patterns, playing on a Victorian design sensibility that sought out a complex interaction of pattern and color.

It is important for the collector of American Indian trade blankets to note that Beacon Manufacturing Company of Swannanoa, North Carolina, was a manufacturer and distributor of Indian-design bedding or camp blankets that were created only for the non-Indian trade. Even though these blankets were, in some cases, similar in appearance to the American Indian trade blanket, they were not designed, produced, or marketed to be wearing blankets or shawls for the American Indian people. Because Beacon did not compete for the American Indian trade, Beacon's blankets, generally a wool-cotton blend, are not considered American Indian trade blankets.

The five major companies that vied for the American Indian trade created an active market among America's native people and achieved their greatest success between 1880 and 1930. In their quest to meet the needs of the American Indian people, these companies stretched the limitations of commercial loom weaving and created blankets in dozens of striking and colorful designs. In order to maximize its marketing, each of the companies made a concerted effort to sell its Indian

trade blankets to a non-Indian market as well. As each company pursued its business goals by supplying the Indian trade, it also helped keep alive the expressive language of the robe.

BUELL BANDED
"COMANCHE"
PATTERN.
THUNDERBIRDS ARE
GOLD ON THE
COLORIZATION SIDE.

CAPPS BANDED "PAPAGO CEREMONIAL" ROBE.

CHAPTER SIX

SECTION THREE
THE MAJOR TRADE BLANKET
MANUFACTURERS

DESIGNS OF THE AMERICAN INDIAN TRADE BLANKET

EACH OF THE COMPANIES INVOLVED IN THE PRODUCTION OF AMERICAN INDIAN TRADE BLANKETS PROMOTED ITS BLANKETS BY EXPLAINING HOW THE DESIGNS ARE TIED TO AMERICAN INDIAN TRADITION. SOME OF THE MORE IMPORTANT DESIGN ELEMENTS LIKE THE CROSS, THE ARROW, AND THE ZIGZAG LINES ARE EASY TO TRACE TO THEIR ROOTS IN NATIVE AMERICAN TRADITION. THE DESIGN CHART INCLUDED IN THIS CHAPTER GIVES SOME INDICATION OF HOW THE DESIGN OF A TRADE BLANKET COULD BE EXPLAINED OR INTERPRETED. MANY OF THESE DESIGNS APPEARED ON TRADITIONAL PERSONAL ITEMS THAT WERE MADE FROM NATURAL MATERIALS AND THEN PAINTED OR DECORATED WITH BEADWORK AND QUILLWORK. OTHER DESIGNS WERE PAINTED ON RAWHIDE CONTAINERS, SUCH AS THE PLAINS *PARFLECHE*, THAT WERE USED TO TRANSPORT AND STORE PERSONAL POSSESSIONS. • THE PAPAGO CEREMONIAL PATTERN (FACING PAGE) PRODUCED BY J. CAPPS AND SONS BETWEEN 1890 AND 1917, PROVIDES AN INTERESTING OPPORTUNITY FOR INTERPRETATION OF TRADE BLANKET DESIGN. ACCORDING TO THE DESIGN ELEMENTS IN THE CHART, THE DOUBLE CROSS ELEMENT THAT RUNS ALONG THE TOP AND BOTTOM OF THE BLANKET IS A SYMBOL FOR A DRAGONFLY. THE TERRACES COULD BE INTERPRETED AS SYMBOLS FOR MOUNTAINS AND THE STRAIGHT LINES EXPLAINED AS SYMBOLS FOR PATHS. THE CROSSES—IN THREE ROWS ALTERNATING WITH the terrace—are symbols for four winds or four directions.

There are accounts from Plains people of the dragonfly as a symbol of life, and there are stories told by members of some tribes that tell of people following swarms of dragonflies—particularly blue dragonflies—because the insects would lead them to water and safety. This lends a specific possibility of a narrative interpretation to the designs in the Papago Ceremonial pattern.

This blanket's pattern could be considered a narrative of a long and even mythic journey across the Plains. The people started the journey following the swarms of dragonflies, symbolized by the rows of double crosses. The straight lines or horizontal stripes tell us that the people followed many trails. The terraces indicate that the people encountered mountains along the trail or perhaps saw them hazy in the distance. The crosses might indicate that there were mountains in all directions or that the people eventually traveled in all four directions.

The design could be interpreted as a narrative progressing from top to bottom or from bottom to top. Or it could be a collection of geometric symbols that provide a sort of shorthand to accompany an oral account of the journey. Some tribal origin myths carry this sort of narrative of a journey from one land to another, sometimes over great distances. The name "Papago Ceremonial" pattern was no doubt simply "assigned" to this blanket by the Capps company. But there is no reason to assume that we can't interpret the design as geometric

THE GREAT CHIEF CHARLOT, FLATHEAD RESERVATION, MONTANA, 1908. HE IS WEARING A BLANKET DRAPED FROM THE WAIST.

poetry.

As for categories of design, there were, and are, six general categories of design for American Indian trade blankets; and the blankets produced by all the major woolen mills, as well as the trade blankets of unknown origin, will generally fit into one of these six categories. The only general production design that is unique to one company is

the Framed design, which was produced only by Pendleton Woolen Mills. Each of the six general styles, as well as many of the individual design elements used in different trade blanket designs, was inspired by a native textile design or a native design element.

TERMINOLOGY FOR BEAD DESIGNS
SOURCE: KROEBER (1908:152); LYFORD (1940:73)

ADDITIONAL DESIGNS WITH TETON DAKOTA NAMES
SOURCE: LYFORD (1940:73-77)

	NAMES ASSIGNED BY KROEBER	NAMES USED BY TETON DAKOTA		
	SPREADING	MOUNTAIN, HILL, CUT-OUT		LIGHTNING
	FORKED	CLOUDS		FILLED UP
	PRONGED	FULL OF POINTS		THREE ROW
	TRIANGLE	TEPEE, ARROW-POINT POINTED		HORSE TRACKS
	DIAMOND	DIAMOND		LEAF
	BOX, SQUARE	BAG		VERTEBRAE
	SQUARE CROSS	STAR, FOUR DIRECTIONS, SQUARE CROSS		HOURGLASS
	FEATHER	FEATHER		TURTLE
	SLANTED BAR			LEAF, POINT
	CROSSED BAR	DRAGON FLY (IF TWO CROSS BARS)		MORNING STAR
	DIAGONAL CHECKER ROW	TWISTED (USUALLY IN THREE OR MORE COLORS)		FOUR DIRECTIONS
	TRIANGULAR STEP, CHECKER PATTERN	MOUNTAIN, HILL, CUT-OUT		SPIDER
	STRIPE, STRIPES	TRAILS		TEPEE
	DRAWN-OUT OR LENGTHENED CHECKER PATTERN	TRIPE		RABBIT EARS
				WHIRLWIND, FEATHER BREATH OF LIFE
				FORKED TREE
				BIRD

From *Hau, Kola! The Plains Indian Collection of the Haffenreffer Museum of Anthropology* by Barbara A. Hail.

STRIPED

One of the earliest and most common patterns used for American Indian trade blankets was the plain Striped blanket. As the name implies, the design consists of plain stripes or groups of stripes with no additional geometric design elements added. A good example of the historic Native American origin of the plain striped blanket is the Zuñi blanket from the School of American Research collection, shown on facing page. Another plain striped blanket of Native American origin is the Navajo First Phase Chief's blanket. These historic blankets were limited to white and one or two colors, usually white and blue, brown, or black. While the simpler striped trade blankets also feature wider stripes of fewer, more distinct colors, many striped blanket designs feature thinner stripes, or stripes of varying widths, grouped by gradations of color.

ANNA CURTIS EAGLENEST (SEATED) WITH UNKNOWN WOMAN, C. 1890s. THESE WOMEN ARE WEARING STRIPED BLANKETS—THE FAVORITE STYLE OF ALMOST EVERY AMERICAN INDIAN TRIBE. (PHOTO COURTESY WESTERN HISTORY COLLECTIONS, UNIVERSITY OF OKLAHOMA LIBRARY)

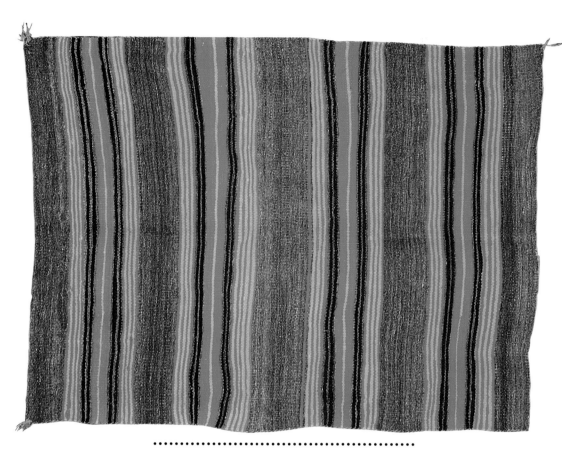

ZUNI STRIPE HAND-WOVEN BLANKET, A VINTAGE
INDIAN BLANKET ON WHICH THE STRIPED TRADE
BLANKET WAS MODELED. (PHOTO COURTESY SCHOOL
OF AMERICAN RESEARCH)

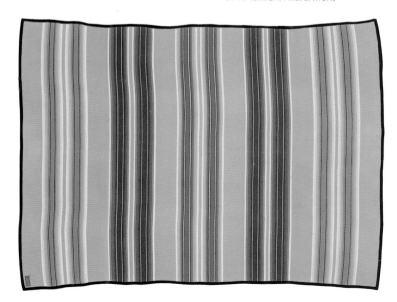

PENDLETON STRIPED
BEAVER STATE ROBE,
1923 LABEL.

PENDLETON STRIPED
SHAWL, 1910–15 PURE
FLEECE WOOL LABEL.

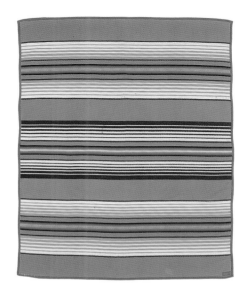

◄ **PENDLETON STRIPED BEAVER STATE ROBE, 1923 LABEL.**

► **PENDLETON STRIPED BEAVER STATE ROBE, C. 1930.**

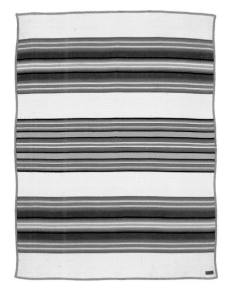

◄ **PENDLETON STRIPED BEAVER STATE ROBE, 1923 LABEL.**

► **PENDLETON STRIPED BEAVER STATE SHAWL, 1923 LABEL.**

BANDED

Another trade blanket design that closely relates to the striped blanket is the Banded blanket, which displays a design that has its roots in early Navajo banded blanket designs. In the simplest banded blankets, the bands include design elements within the bands—not simply stripes.

An example of the influences that resulted in this design is the Second Phase Chief's blanket in which the geometric design elements—usually rectangles—are regularly spaced within the stripes that dominate the pattern.

TWO OSAGE WOMEN WEARING BANDED STYLE SHAWLS
(BOTH POSSIBLY RACINE BLANKETS). (PHOTO COURTESY
THE THOMAS GILCREASE INSTITUTE OF AMERICAN HISTORY
AND ART, TULSA, OK))

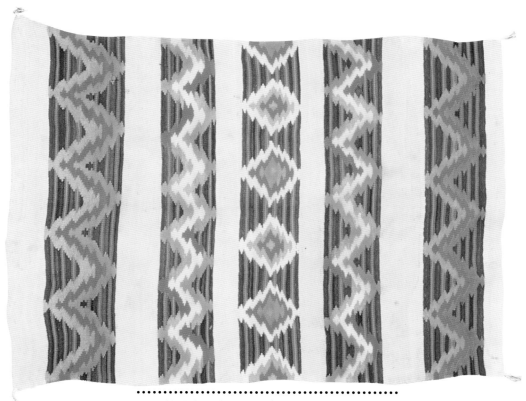

NAVAJO BANDED HAND-WOVEN BLANKET, THE
INSPIRATION FOR THE BANDED TRADE BLANKETS.
(PHOTO COURTESY SCHOOL OF AMERICAN RESEARCH)

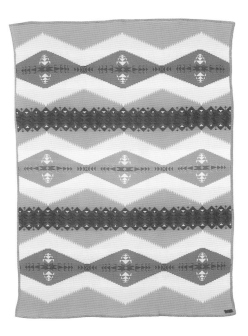

◄ PENDLETON BANDED
ROBE, C. 1920s.

◄ PENDLETON BANDED
ROBE, 1910 CATALOG.

**PENDLETON BANDED
BEAVER STATE SHAWL,
C. 1920s.**

**PENDLETON BANDED
BEAVER STATE SHAWL,
C. 1920s.**

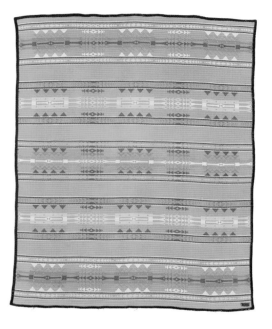

◀
**PENDLETON BANDED
BEAVER STATE ROBE,
1923 LABEL.**

▶
**PENDLETON BANDED
BEAVER STATE ROBE,
C. 1920s.**

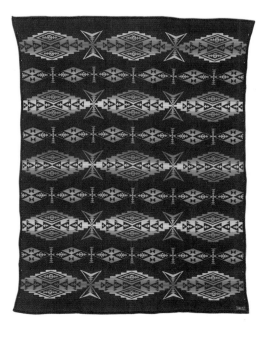

◀
**PENDLETON BANDED
ROBE, C. 1920s.**

▶
**PENDLETON BANDED
BEAVER STATE ROBE,
C. 1920s.**

CENTER POINT

The Center Point pattern blanket contains a central design element that dominates the blanket's overall design. The major design elements always fall within a broad band across the center of the blanket. Even though most Center Point blankets feature only one dominant design element, sometimes identical design elements are repeated within the central band.

JUAN CRUZ, SAN ILDEFONSO PUEBLO, C. 1935, WEARING A
PENDLETON CENTER POINT BLANKET, C. 1920S. (PHOTO BY
T. HARMON PARKHURST, COURTESY MUSEUM OF NEW
MEXICO, NEG. 9195)

54

NAVAJO CENTER
POINT HAND-WOVEN
RUG, AN INSPIRATION
FOR THE CENTER
POINT DESIGN TRADE
BLANKETS. (PHOTO
COURTESY SCHOOL OF
AMERICAN RESEARCH)

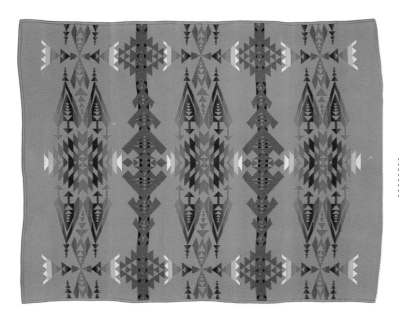

PENDLETON
CENTER POINT ROBE,
C. 1920s–30s.

PENDLETON
CENTER POINT ROBE,
1921 LABEL.

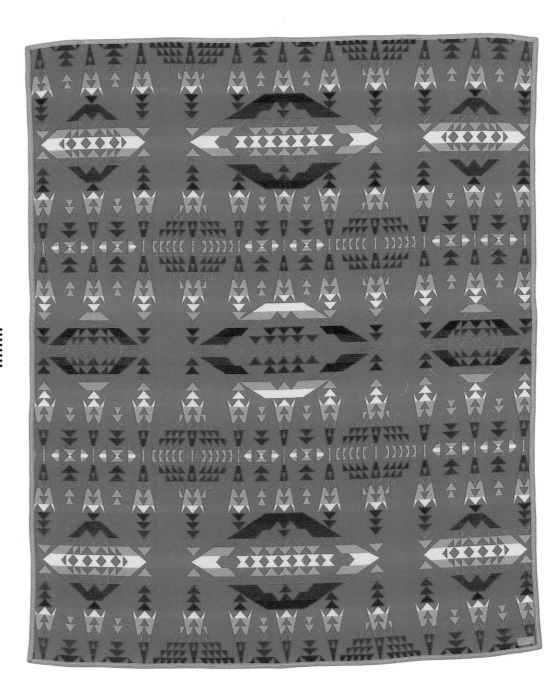

◄ **PENDLETON CENTER POINT ROBE, C. 1920s–30s.**

► **PENDLETON CENTER POINT ROBE, C. 1920s–30s.**

◄ **PENDLETON CENTER POINT ROBE, C. 1920s–30s.**

► **PENDLETON CENTER POINT ROBE, C. 1920s–30s.**

FRAMED

———

The Framed blanket, unique to the Pendleton Woolen Mills, has its design origins in the Rio Grande weavings. Each Framed blanket design features four major elements—one in each corner of the frame. The "frame" varies in width but is almost always at least twelve inches wide.

RIO GRANDE HISPANIC FRAMED WEAVING, A HISTORIC MODEL FOR THE FRAMED TRADE BLANKETS. (PHOTO COURTESY SCHOOL OF AMERICAN RESEARCH)

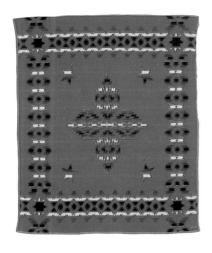

◄ PENDLETON FRAMED ROBE, C. 1915–21.

► PENDLETON FRAMED BEAVER STATE ROBE, C. 1920S–30S.

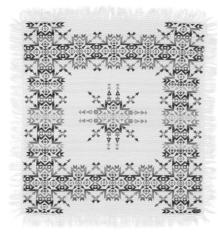

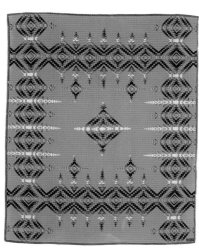

◄ PENDLETON BEAVER STATE FRAMED SHAWL, C. 1915–23.

► PENDLETON FRAMED ROBE, C. 1915–21.

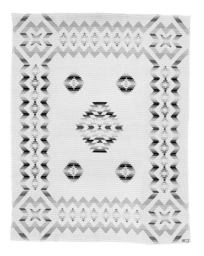

◄ PENDLETON BEAVER STATE FRAMED ROBE, C. 1920s.

► PENDLETON FRAMED ROBE, C. 1920s.

OVERALL

—

The Overall blanket design repeats a pattern over the entire weaving. Again, one can see similar overall designs in historic Navajo blankets in which a pattern, often including serrated stripes, terraces, or diamonds, is repeated with a regular spacing all the way to the edge of the weaving.

NAVAJO OVERALL RUG, A HISTORIC MODEL FOR OVERALL
TRADE BLANKETS. (PHOTO COURTESY SCHOOL OF
AMERICAN RESEARCH)

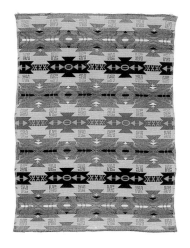

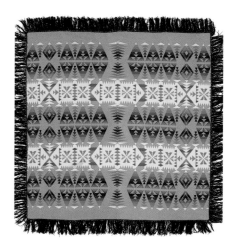

◄ PENDLETON OVERALL
"SWASTIKA" ROBE,
C. 1920s.

► PENDLETON OVERALL
SHAWL, C. 1920s.

◄ PENDLETON OVERALL
ROBE, C. 1920s.

► PENDLETON OVERALL
ROBE, 1910 CATALOG.

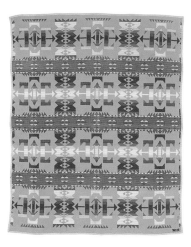

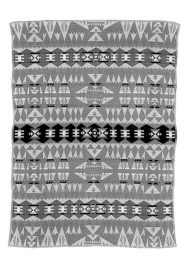

◄ PENDLETON OVERALL
ROBE, C. 1920s.

► PENDLETON OVERALL
ROBE, C. 1920s.

NINE ELEMENT

The Nine Element trade blanket design features three rows of three design elements. The design continues to the edge of the blanket, with a partial design element on the blanket's edge, so the parallel rows of three design elements along either edge of the blanket show only partial design elements.

The central panel of three design elements, parallel to the edge panels, contains complete design elements. The Third Phase Navajo Chief's blanket design, with its nine dominant geometric design elements, is the historic predecessor of the Nine Element trade blanket design.

NINE ELEMENT BLANKET. (PHOTO BY T. HARMON PARKHURST, COURTESY MUSEUM OF NEW MEXICO, NEG. 46072)

THIRD PHASE NAVAJO
CHIEF'S BLANKET WITH
A NINE ELEMENT
PATTERN, PROBABLY
A MODEL FOR NINE
ELEMENT TRADE
BLANKETS. (PHOTO
COURTESY SCHOOL OF
AMERICAN RESEARCH)

◄
PENDLETON NINE
ELEMENT ROBE,
C. 1920s.

►
PENDLETON NINE
ELEMENT BEAVER STATE
SHAWL, COPYRIGHT 1923
LABEL.

PENDLETON NINE
ELEMENT ROBE,
C. 1920s.

PENDLETON NINE
ELEMENT ROBE,
1921 LABEL.

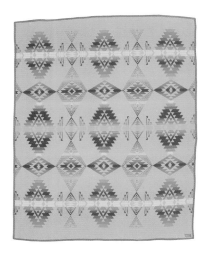

◄ PENDLETON NINE
ELEMENT ROBE,
1921 LABEL.

► PENDLETON NINE
ELEMENT ROBE,
1921 LABEL.

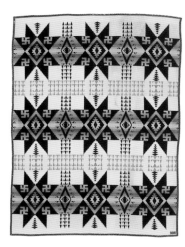

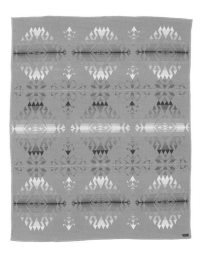

◄ PENDLETON NINE
ELEMENT "SWASTIKA"
ROBE, C. 1920s.

► PENDLETON NINE
ELEMENT ROBE,
C. 1920s.

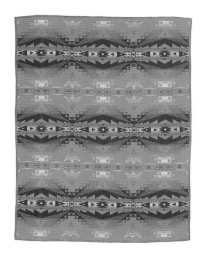

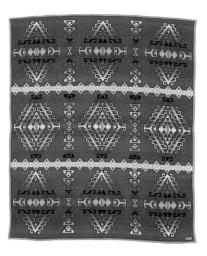

◄ PENDLETON NINE
ELEMENT ROBE,
1921 LABEL.

► PENDLETON NINE
ELEMENT ROBE,
1921 LABEL.

Six Element

Another design that is related to Nine Element blanket design is the Six Element design. The six element could be called a recessive nine element, depending on the placement of the elements. The six elements are placed in a pattern similar to that on the Nine Element blankets, but, as the name states, there are three fewer elements.

PATRICIO CALABAZA, SANTO DOMINGO PUEBLO, WEARING
A SIX ELEMENT PENDLETON ROBE, C. 1920S. (SEE SIX
ELEMENT PENDLETON BLANKET ON FACING PAGE)
(PHOTO COURTESY MUSEUM OF NEW MEXICO, NEG. 4302)

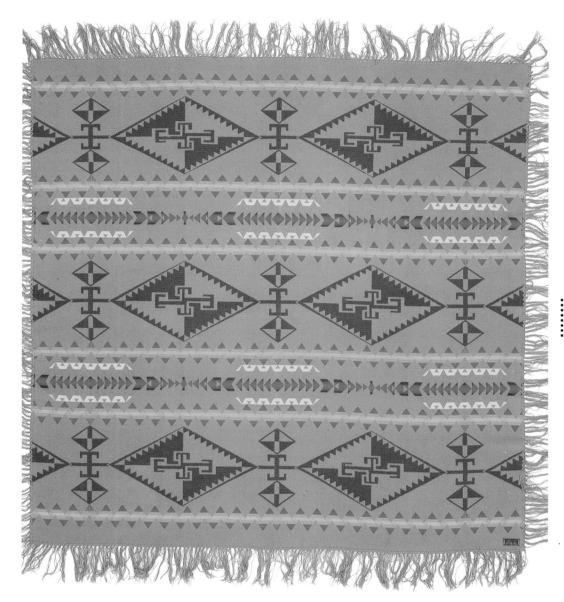

PENDLETON SIX
ELEMENT SHAWL,
1921 LABEL.

PENDLETON NINE
ELEMENT ROBE,
1921 LABEL.

When analyzing the pattern of an American Indian trade blanket, first determine the background color. On all but the most complex Striped blanket design patterns, one ground color will stand out. As you examine the blanket, imagine that the design is actually a separate element laid down over the background color. Once you see the design clearly stand out against the background, it will be easier to analyze. In some trade blankets with complex designs, the design might appear to fit into more than one design category. In these cases, begin by choosing the dominant design elements, the ones to which your eye is first drawn. For example, when looking at a Nine Element design, one could conclude that the design is a Banded design because the nine major design elements fall within broad bands. However, the Nine Element design is the dominant of the two designs. This analysis will be a great help not only in developing an appreciation for the complexity of trade blanket color and design, but also in identifying blankets of unknown origin.

As for the individual designers who created the blanket designs, only one achieved individual fame. His name was Joe Rawnsley and he worked for Pendleton Mills for twenty-eight years, between 1901 and 1929. Rawnsley spent months at a time with several tribes, traveling extensively around the United States. He shared the day-to-day lives of the Indian people and learned directly from Indian informants about the specific traditional designs and their importance.

A popular but controversial element that appears in many early trade blan-ket designs is the swastika, or whirling logs design. The swastika was commonly known as a sign of good luck and was adopted by such different organizations as a New Mexico coal company and the University of New Mexico, which published a yearbook called *The Swastika* before World War II. The Fred Harvey Company also incorporated the swastika into its jewelry designs. While the swastika has been given several names, including the Navajo "whirling logs," its origins goes at least as far back as the Anasazi people—the Ancient Ones—of what is now the southwestern United States. Anasazi drawings of the swastika can be seen in the Antelope Ruins site. In the ancient uses, it may have been a symbol of the four winds or the four directions. The Buell Manufacturing Company produced a striking blanket design called the Moki, which featured a swastika in each corner of the blanket. The catalog description says the Moki is "a robe designed to meet the popular demand for the Swastika Cross, the good luck sign. This design signifies 'a big camp with many tents, water, and good luck.'" It is unfortunate that there is such an overpowering negative association with the whirling logs design, because it creates a dramatic visual impact, particularly when combined with strong colors as in the blanket designs created by Capps, Buell and others.

When presenting the trade blankets to the non-Indian market, each company designated individual blanket designs with names of Native American origin—often the designs were given tribal names. These names were given

BUELL "MOKI"
(SWASTIKA PATTERN),
C. 1912.

to the same blankets sold to the American Indian people, but the Indian people responded more to the color, design, and quality of the blanket itself. The names were assigned more for poetic impact than with a specific regard for accuracy. For example, the Shoshoni design produced by Buell Manufacturing Company is a distinctly Navajo regional weaving design woven in the traditional colors. Even though the names assigned to the trade blankets were inaccurate, they are convenient for collectors today because they provide a foolproof way to identify and classify the historic trade blankets.

The descriptions of design origins that appear in the individual company catalogs are full of enthusiastic, romanticized distortion. The 1910 Pendleton catalog says:

Picture the West in all its wealth of color and grandeur; conceive if you can the Indian craftsman at his loom, weaving in his crude yet dexterous way his ideas of textile art. To him is all the credit due for the beautiful patterns and the unique color combinations of the famous Pendleton Line. The skillful designers and weavers of the Pendleton Woolen Mills have simply transformed the original designs and colorings into a more refined form.

This passage is confusing at best, because it gives no specific information about the origin of any individual design elements or the overall textile

BUELL "SHOSHONI"
PATTERN, 1912
CATALOG. THIS
ILLUSTRATES BUELL'S
ATTEMPT TO
DUPLICATE
NAVAJO RUGS.

designs. In fact, many of the design elements are more like the painted decorations on rawhide containers or beaded designs from Plains tribes that had no weaving tradition at all. In the 1927 catalog, Pendleton gives a more accurate description of the design process.

"These Indian blankets were originated *for* the Indian—not by him." But there is some confusion tossed into the next sentence: "With his own crude methods of weaving, the Indian could not reproduce the intricate designs and elaborate color combinations sufficiently to interpret his inherent art in a blanket of first quality." In direct contradiction to this, Navajo women actually can add more colors to a single horizontal line on their vertical loom weavings than the commercial manufacturing companies can add to a trade blanket.

All American Indian trade blankets are woven on looms that allow for two colors on any individual row; the designs have a positive and negative side. The result of this double-shuttle loom allows the viewer to visualize the design more completely on one side— the "patternization side"—on which the pattern is most distinct. On the reverse of the patternization side is the "colorization side," on which the visual impact of the trade blanket's colors outweighs the visual impact of the design. Often, the dominant designs that are sharper on the pattern side appear to be recessive, or even lost in the colors of the colorization side. In many trade blankets, these designs and colors often appear to be overlaid on a field of a single dominant background color.

In identifying trade blanket patterns, it is useful to remember that the company label generally appears on the pattern side of the blanket. For convenience, consider the side of the blanket on which the label appears as the "A"

side. On a trade blanket manufactured by Pendleton or Capps, you'll find that the "A" side of the blanket is the pattern side. Oregon City, on the other hand, attached its labels to the colorization side of the blanket. So, for an Oregon City blanket, the "A" side—the side on which the label is sewn—is the colorization side.

In their American Indian trade blankets, each manufacturer used striking color combinations to create amazingly complex, and often unique, patterns. In their efforts to develop ever more exciting designs for their American Indian customers, these manufacturers redefined the limits of commercial weaving.

In this chapter, we've established the six broad categories of trade blanket designs not only to facilitate identification of the blankets but also to enhance the enjoyment of the blankets themselves. Even though identifying the characteristic designs will help the collector track down a blanket's origin, it should also lead to a greater appreciation of the intricacy of each blanket's color and design on a purely sensory level. Look closely at the blankets pictured in the book, then imagine how the colors and patterns come swirling to life when worn by a dancer.

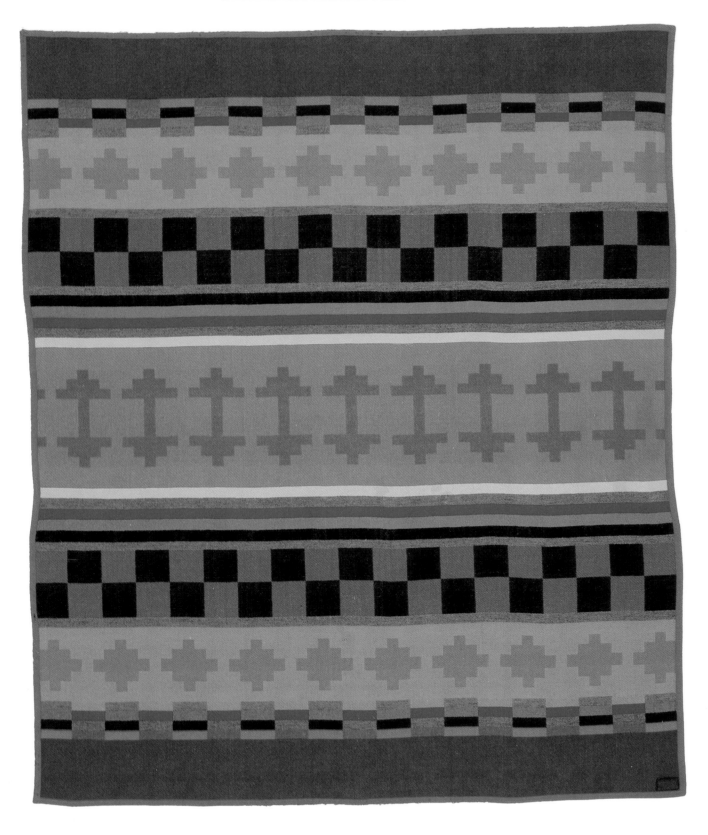

CAPPS BANDED "SHOSHONE" PATTERN, 1913 CATALOG.

THE CAPPS INDIAN BLANKET

"A Dream of the Far Prairie"

CAPPS' 1913 CATALOG USED A PHOTOGRAPH OF BUFFALO BILL AND A GROUP OF INDIANS WEARING CAPPS BLANKETS.

I AM PLEASED TO SAY, THAT FOR CHARACTERISTIC INDIAN DESIGNS, BEAUTY AND BRILLIANCY OF COLOR, AND FOR QUALITY, THE "CAPPS INDIAN" BLANKET IS SUPERIOR TO ANY BLANKET THAT I AM ACQUAINTED WITH, MADE FOR THE INDIAN TRADE.

COLONEL WM. F. "BUFFALO BILL" CODY
JULY 28, 1911

BY 1911, BUFFALO BILL'S WILD WEST SHOW HAD CAPTURED THE IMAGINATIONS OF ROMANTICS AROUND THE WORLD. BUFFALO BILL CODY MAXIMIZED THE DRAMATIC, WORLD-WIDE SUCCESS OF HIS WILD WEST EXTRAVAGANZA BY AMPLIFYING THE POPULAR, ROMANTIC MYTHS OF THE NINETEENTH-CENTURY AMERICAN WEST AND THE AMERICAN INDIAN AS NOBLE SAVAGE. TAPPING INTO THE SAME VEIN OF ROMANTICISM, J. CAPPS AND SONS INFORMED ALL NON-INDIAN CUSTOMERS THAT TO WRAP UP IN A WARM AND COLORFUL CAPPS BLANKET WAS TO REALIZE "A DREAM OF THE FAR PRAIRIE AND A COVERED FIRE." BUFFALO BILL CODY'S WORDS IN THE CAPPS 1911 CATALOG TESTIFY NOT ONLY TO THE quality of the Capps Indian blanket, but also to the marketing acumen of the firm that promoted itself as "Blanket Makers to the Indian Tribes."

Capps' 1911 catalog intrigued its readers with a photograph of Colonel Cody himself surrounded by his Indian employees—wearing feather head-dresses and wrapped in Capps blankets. Homebound readers back East could see the striking patterns created by the riotous blend of reds, blues, and

JACK WHEET-SOOT
OF THE CAYUSE
TRIBE WEARING A
CAPPS BLANKET.
(PHOTO BY MAJOR
LEE MOORHOUSE,
COURTESY UNIVERSITY
OF OREGON LIBRARY)

oranges in the blankets modeled by the Wild West Show's Native American actors. To acquire a Capps blanket and display it in your home was to own a piece of the vanishing romance of the American West and to achieve the blissful harmony of the Noble Red Man...or that's what the advertising promised.

This Capps-enhanced mystique waxed eloquent about "a true Romance, written in flaming color all over our

land—the story of a race ever taking the long trail toward the setting sun, fighting every step and leaving behind the imperishable and heroic history of a lost cause."

And this mystique was personified (and, in the readers' eyes, legitimized) by Buffalo Bill and his myth-making colleague Pawnee Bill. By the time Capps enlisted these remarkable show-men to breathe life into the advertising plan, the firm had been manufacturing blankets for the Indian trade for almost twenty-five years. An article in the *Mutual News* from November 1910 reminded the reader that

for more than twenty years, a noteworthy item of manufacture has been the Art Indian blankets, of which thousands have been made every year and distributed to the scattered Indian tribes of the West through the agency of the Indian traders.

The 1913 catalog explains, "We began more than a generation ago making blankets for the Indians for their own wear on the reservations."

If the Capps marketing plan—complete with Buffalo Bill and purple prose—was flamboyant, it was not a reflection of the firm's founder himself. The embodiment of the pioneer Protestant work ethic, Joseph Capps built a solid business on a foundation of thrift and ingenuity. In 1839, before he was thirty, Capps established a wool carding operation in Jacksonville, Illinois, and over the years enlarged his carding operation to include spinning. By 1852 he had added looms and weaving machinery in order to manu-facture cloth. The expansion into new merchandise continued, and by the mid-1880s J. Capps and Sons Limited enjoyed an impressive annual revenue of more than $200,000 from sales of clothing, cloth, and blankets.

No doubt the idea of catering to a controlled market in the Indian trade appealed to the Capps business sense. Between 1890 and 1917, Capps attributed "an important volume of business" to the manufacture of blankets for sale to federal Indian agents on western reservations. Even so, the history of the firm published in its centennial year of 1939 offers less than one of its twenty-nine pages to the discussion of the Indian blanket business. In addition to the mention of the trade with federal agents, the catalog says that "for a time the mill advertised these blankets in publications of national circulation and sold them direct to individuals." Then the discussion quickly moves on to trousers and other products sold to the U.S. government during the First World War.

The 1874 *United States Textile Manufacturer's Directory* described Capps as working with "4 sets of cards." Dockham's 1884 directory described the firm's capacity as "7 sets cards, 33 looms, steam power." All used in the manufacture of "flannels, cassimeres, blankets, yarn." Seven years later, Dockham's 1891 publication showed that Capps still had seven sets cards but had expanded to fifty looms. After the turn of the century, the 1905 directory showed the company with the same number of cards but fewer looms— thirty-six. By 1927, Capps was out of the trade-blanket business, concentrating on Indian blanket mackinaws, a variety of heavy wool coat with popular trade blanket designs primarily for the non-Indian market.

True to his conservative ways ("Don't keep all your eggs in one basket!"), Capps maintained a diversified product line. Unlike the other mills that produced only blankets for the Indian trade, Capps manufactured a complete line of woolen goods, including trousers and fabric. Also unlike other mills, Capps restricted its Indian trade to the central United States, closer to the home office. It was only in its attempt to reach the non-Indian market

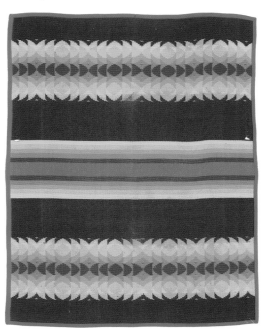

CAPPS BANDED, UNKNOWN PATTERN, C. 1913.

that Capps and Sons advertised nationally in publications like the 1910 *Delineator*.

Even though the Indian trade was given only a brief mention in the firm's centennial story, it is the American Indian trade blankets for which Capps will be remembered. The company produced twenty-two distinct designs in more than two hundred different color combinations. All blankets were

Genuine Indian Blankets for Your Home

THERE is nothing so beautiful—so warm—so cheery—as a genuine Indian Blanket or two. Women prize them more than any other single decoration in their homes. They are a mark of luxury—of refinement—of taste.

In the living-room, boudoir, on the porch or in the automobile or carriage—they have a hundred and one useful purposes, as couch covers, draperies, throws, athletic blankets, bath-robes, steamer rugs, et cetera.

A generation ago we began making Blankets for the Navajo, Cheyenne, Comanche, Sioux and other tribes. These Blankets became famous. The Indians sold them for fabulous prices. To-day they are found in the homes of the most aristocratic people who appreciate the beautiful.

The Blankets at your dealer's with the Capps mark are identical with those that go to the Indian agencies—except that they are clean, sanitary, sweet. They're made of pure wool, generous in size, brilliant in their fast colors.

The Best Dealers Sell These Blankets

We buy the wool, dye, spin and weave it in our own looms.

We know it is pure.

The Blankets are a riot of colors, or subdued shades, as you prefer.

The designs are authentic—more than 200—in plain stripes or fancy figures.

The color combinations are innumerable. These Blankets are 60 in. x 72 in. The dyes are fast; the colors will not run nor fade in any ordinary usage. Can be washed like all woolens.

We and the Dealer Guarantee Them

If your dealer has not the genuine, guaranteed Blanket, we will tell you of one who has. Or—

Send us his name and the price—$7.50—and we will send you the Blanket by prepaid express.

Be sure to state your color preferences, and whether you want stripes or fancy figures—the brilliant blankets of the Northern tribes, or the more subdued hues of the Southwestern Indians. We will ship immediately, subject to your examination and approval.

NOTE TO DEALER: We have a most interesting proposition for you. A postal will bring it to you.

Give Him One
for
His den
To use in camp
A lounging robe
An automobile robe

J. CAPPS & SONS MODERN MILLS

Give Her One
for
A throw
Porch rug
Her boudoir
A bath-robe

Be assured it will be the most acceptable Christmas gift one can receive.

J. CAPPS & SONS, Ltd.

Spinners of pure wool since 1839

JACKSONVILLE, ILL.

the standard sixty inches by seventy-two inches and weighed three pounds. Each Capps design was distinguished by the name of a Native American tribe—not that the patterns really had much to do with the tribes for which they were named. Even though the names given them weren't specifically applicable, the vivid Capps blankets

had been designed for the Indian trade. There wasn't a need for colorful catalogs and magazine ads because the Indian traders and Indian agencies enjoyed a captive market. Yet there was some attempt to customize the product so that it would better fit the needs of the Indian customer. The Capps blanket designs were somewhat simpler

◄ PAGE FROM 1913 CAPPS CATALOG SHOWS A "PONCA SWASTIKA" PATTERN.

► PAGE FROM 1913 CAPPS CATALOG ILLUSTRATING AN "APACHE LIGHTNING" DESIGN.

◄ PAGE FROM 1913 CAPPS CATALOG ILLUSTRATING THE "MOHAWK WAR STRIPE" PATTERN.

► PAGE FROM 1913 CAPPS CATALOG SHOWING THE "CHEYENNE BASKET" PATTERN BLANKET.

than those of other mills. In fact, the Capps designs could have been produced on a basic vertical loom as there were few zigzag or curvilinear designs. Most of the Capps designs were simple vertical and serrated patterns.

Capps published catalogs picturing its line of trade blankets and advertised a unique opportunity for the public to obtain these authentic items directly from the manufacturer. The catalogs were accompanied by national magazine advertisements featuring the Cozy Corner Girl, a fictitious spokeswoman who related her life's story in terms of the Capps blankets that made her life meaningful. The 1911 price for Capps Indian blankets was $7.50.

Capps also wanted its blankets to appeal to "The Tribe of the Great Outdoors" and explained that the blankets were 100 percent pure fleece wool, both warp and weft (or "warp and woof," as the promotional material said). This appeal was made more specific with claims that the blanket designs were "Indian art" adapted from Indian designs.

Since many of the company records were destroyed when Capps was sold, we don't know exactly the research that went into the selection of patterns. The 1911 catalog says, "Navajos and Southwest tribes prefer harmonizing colors. Northern Indians insist on vivid contrast." This passage indicates that the Capps researchers were concerned about the specific aesthetic sense of the individual tribes. But, if we can judge by a 1912 ad in *The Delineator*, the Capps concern for the individual tribes was more one of embellishing the firm's marketing success. That ad tells its customers they have a choice "from the gorgeous conception of the warlike Shoshone and the dazzling colors of the Kiowa to the harmonious tones of the Osage and the restful hues of the Navajo."

A brief glance through one of the Capps catalogs proves that the Capps advertising staff used the names of tribes primarily for poetic impact. For example, the Ponca Swastika was described as "the Legendary Mystical Figure," or the Apache Lightning design as "a beautiful, Striking Motif."

Capps produced more blanket designs that incorporated the whirling logs, or swastika, element in its blankets than other firms did. Of course, when Capps was designing and producing its blankets, the swastika had yet to take on the negative connotations given it after World War II.

At the time Capps and Sons published its catalogs in 1911 and 1913, it was the "golden age" of the Indian trade blanket. A few years later, during the First World War, the Capps machinery was turned over to the manufacture of army blankets, trousers, and other products for the war effort. There would never be another Kiowa Rattlesnake design blanket made for any market—Indian or white.

FOR THE COLLECTOR OF CAPPS BLANKETS

I. SIZES AND WEIGHT:

In the 1911 Capps catalog, one reads, "Capps Indian Blankets are uniform in size, weight, and quality. Every one is 60 x 72 inches, which is the standard Indian blanket size. It weighs a full three pounds, is all wool, and is always of superlative weave and worth."

II. NOTES ON CONSTRUCTION OF CAPPS WEAVINGS:

The Capps Company produced blankets, or robes, only. There are no examples of fringed shawls produced by J. Capps and Sons.

III. LABELS:

History shows at least three distinct label styles.

1 1/2" X 1"
FIRST CAPPS LABEL, "J. CAPPS AND SONS, LTD., WOOLEN MILLS, ESTABLISHED 1839"

2" X 1 3/8"
SECOND CAPPS LABEL, "J. CAPPS AND SONS, LTD., WOOLEN MILLS, ESTABLISHED 1839"

2 1/4" X 1 1/2"
THIRD CAPPS LABEL, "J. CAPPS AND SONS, LTD., WOOLEN MILLS, ESTABLISHED 1839," UNLIKE THE FIRST TWO LABELS, THE LARGE C HAS NO SCROLL WORK.

DETAIL OF CAPPS LOGO FROM 1913 CATALOG.

IV. BINDING OF THE CAPPS TRADE BLANKETS:

Capps blankets generally feature a red felt binding, although there are examples of brown felt bindings. There are two rows of stitching that attach the binding to the blanket.

DETAIL OF CAPPS FELT BINDING.

INTERIOR OF
GOVERNOR LENTE'S
HOME, ISLETA PUEBLO,
C. 1905. THE MAN IS
WEARING A CAPPS
"KIOWA RATTLESNAKE"
DESIGN BLANKET.
(PHOTO COURTESY
MUSEUM OF NEW
MEXICO, NEG. 12331)

CAPPS BANDED
"KIOWA RATTLESNAKE"
ROBE, 1913 CATALOG.

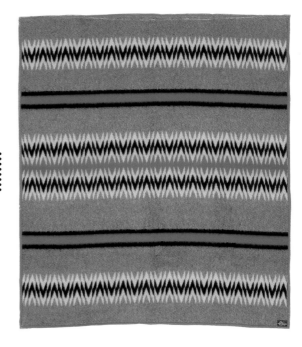

NAVAJO FAMILY,
SHIPROCK AGENCY
MAN IN CENTER IS
WEARING A CAPPS
"NAVAJO BASKET-
WEAVE," C. 1910. NOTE
THE THREE DIFFERENT
WEARING STYLES.
(PHOTO COURTESY
MUSEUM OF NEW
MEXICO, NEG. 42217)

CAPPS BANDED
"NAVAJO BASKET-
WEAVE" ROBE, 1913
CATALOG.

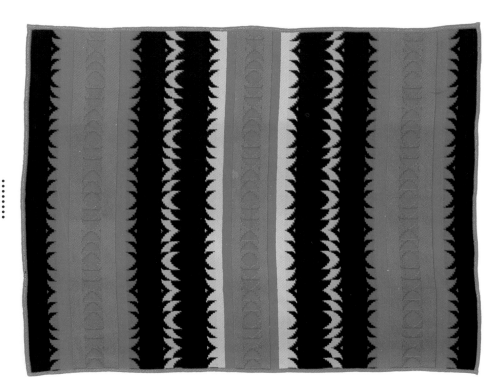

CAPPS BANDED,
UNKNOWN PATTERN,
DATE UNKNOWN.

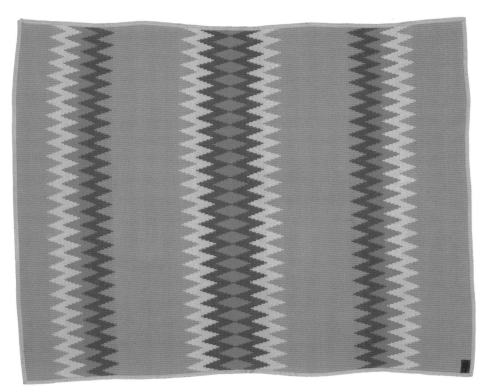

CAPPS BANDED
"APACHE LIGHTNING"
ROBE, 1913 CATALOG.

◄ CAPPS BANDED "COMANCHE" ROBE, 1913 CATALOG.

► CAPPS BANDED "NAVAJO SYMBOLIC FIGURES" ROBE, 1913 CATALOG.

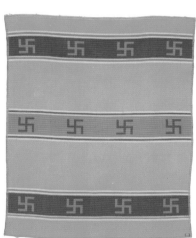

◄ CAPPS STRIPED, UNKNOWN PATTERN, C. 1910s.

► CAPPS BANDED "PONCA SWASTIKA" ROBE, 1913 CATALOG.

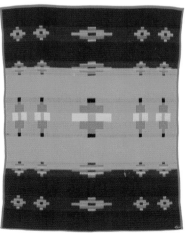

◄ CAPPS BANDED "NAVAJO BASKET WEAVE" ROBE, 1913 CATALOG.

► CAPPS BANDED "MOQI" ROBE, 1913 CATALOG.

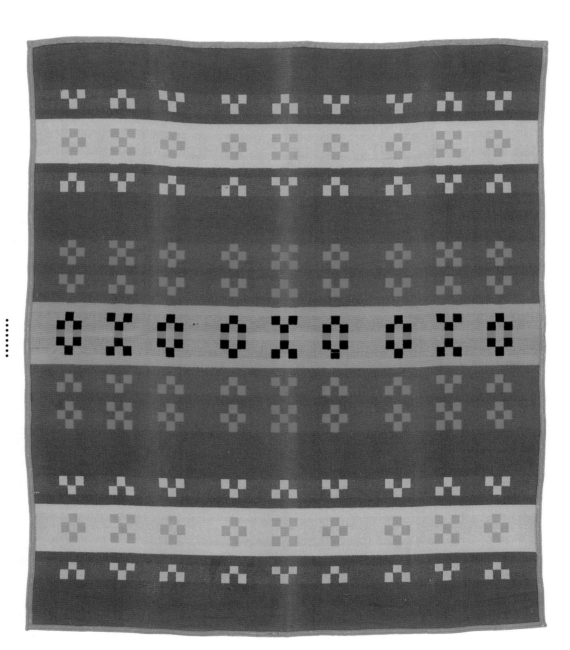

CAPPS BANDED
ROBE, UNKNOWN
PATTERN.

CAPPS BANDED
"KLAMATH SWASTIKA
STRIPE" ROBE, 1913
CATALOG.

CAPPS BANDED
"ARAPAHOE
ARROWHEAD" ROBE,
1913 CATALOG.

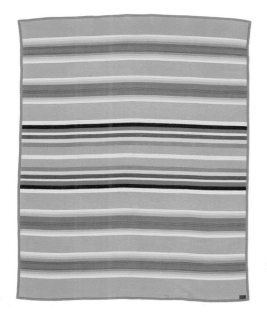

CAPPS STRIPED "OSAGE"
PATTERN, 1913 CATALOG.

CAPPS BANDED
"HUALPAI" ROBE,
1913 CATALOG.

OREGON CITY BANDED (CROSSED ARROW) ROBE, FEATURED
IN 1911 CATALOG.

OREGON CITY WOOLEN MILLS

"PERFECTLY WOVEN 'NAVAJO ART-CRAFT' FABRICS"

THE 1894 EDITION OF THE *OREGONIAN'S HANDBOOK OF THE PACIFIC NORTHWEST* DOCUMENTS THE IMPORTANCE OF THE FALLS OF THE WILLAMETTE RIVER. AT THIS POINT, THE HANDBOOK EXPLAINS, THE RIVER "POURS ITS GREAT VOLUME OF WATER OVER A LEDGE OF BASALTIC ROCK MAKING A VERTICAL DROP OF 42 FEET." BECAUSE OF THIS NATURAL WATER POWER, THE FALLS ARE NATURAL "AS SITES FOR LARGE AND SUBSTANTIAL MANUFACTURING PLANTS." AT THIS SITE, THE "NIAGARA OF THE WEST," THE OREGON CITY WOOLEN MILLS WAS FOUNDED AND GREW INTO ONE OF THE MAJOR PRODUERS OF AMERICAN INDIAN TRADE BLANKETS. • IN THE LAST FEW WEEKS OF 1862, A GROUP OF OREGON CITY'S PROMINENT CITIZENS FORMED A COMMITTEE TO EXPLORE THE OPTIONS FOR DEVELOPING A WOOLEN MILL FOR THE SITE THAT HAD PREVIOUSLY BEEN OCCUPIED ONLY BY A SMALL GRIST MILL. ON CHRISTMAS EVE, SPECIFIC PLANS WERE MADE TO PURCHASE PROPERTY AND SELL STOCK TO RAISE THE APPROXIMATELY $75,000 NEEDED TO DEVELOP A WOOLEN MILL. A FEW DAYS LATER, SIXTEEN MEN BECAME THE ORIGINAL INCORPORATORS OF THE OREGON CITY WOOLEN MANUFACTURING COMPANY. • THE ORIGINAL STOCK OFFERING WAS FOR $60,000 TO BE RAISED AT $100 PER SHARE. EVEN THOUGH $30,000 WAS RAISED IN ONLY THREE DAYS, THERE WAS LITTLE SIGNIFICANT ACTION TAKEN TO BEGIN CONSTRUCTION OF THE PLANT FOR SEVERAL MONTHS.

TEOFOLD ORETEGA, TESUQUE PUEBLO, WEARING OREGON CITY BLANKET C. 1920. (PHOTO BY T. HARMON PARKHURST, COURTESY MUSEUM OF NEW MEXICO, NEG. 47270)

It was agreed that no additional action would be taken until the entire $60,000 was raised. After the initial flurry of activity, cautious investors and a general scarcity of capital slowed the fund-raising significantly. Another part of the problem that caused the delay was a dispute over rights to the Willamette River's power and access to the land adjacent to the river. After a lengthy dispute, a resolution was made and the company was reincorporated as the Oregon City Manufacturing Company in February 1864. At that time, the incorporators decided that the company needed a building large enough to house ten sets of carding machines. As fortune had it, the Oregon City mill was able to hire L. E. Pratt, formerly of the Willamette Woolen Mills in Salem, to manage the operation.

By the time Pratt had purchased the mill machinery for $20,000 and paid $7,000 to have it shipped to Oregon City, an additional $32,000 had been allocated for the mill's building and $10,000 invested in location and water rights. A total of $73,000, just shy of the projected $75,000, was required to get the mill up and running.

Even though there is contradictory information about how successful the Oregon City mill was in its first year, it was definitely busy from the beginning and, by 1866, when L. E. Pratt resigned his position, the mill was known to produce some of the finest woolen products on the market. The mill had expanded steadily and employed eight people and processed three hundred thousand pounds of wool annually. During 1866, Ralph Jacobs first became associated with the company as vice-president and, later in the year, as managing agent.

Jacobs was listed as managing agent in the 1874 *United States Textile Manufacturer's Directory*, which stated that the mill housed six sets of cards and twenty-four looms. The *Dockham's American Report and Directory of the Textile Manufacture and Dry Goods Trade* for

1891–92, listed Ralph Jacobs as president and agent and J. Jacobs as treasurer and superintendent of the plant that had thirteen sets of cards and forty-nine broad looms. The same report also listed Jacobs Brothers & Company of Portland as one of the $400,000 company's selling agents. In the 1904–05 *Blue Book Textile Directory*, Oregon City operated fourteen sets of cards, sixteen broad looms and forty-two of the smaller capacity narrow looms. In *Davison's Textile Blue Book* for 1927–28, the mill worked with the same number of cards but had grown to 114 broad looms.

Ralph Jacobs, along with his brother Isaac, increased his investment in the mill and guided it through years of expansion and serious labor conflicts that developed with the Ku Klux Klan as a result of the mill's hiring of Chinese workers. In spite of labor trouble and an uneven market, the Oregon City mill continued to produce award-winning woolen products. By 1870, Jacobs was joined on the Oregon City Woolen Mills board of directors by his brother. There are differing accounts concerning the pace at which the Jacobs brothers gained possession of the mill. One version says they were sole owners by 1867. Either way, they owned the mill by 1872.

And in that year, 1872, the Oregon City mill was destroyed by fire, with total damages reaching $250,000. Even though insurance covered only $65,000 of the loss, the Jacobs brothers refinanced the mill and were back in operation by mid-1873. This tenacious commitment to rebuild the Oregon City mill from a total loss was typical Jacobs brothers' spirit. (The 1872 fire

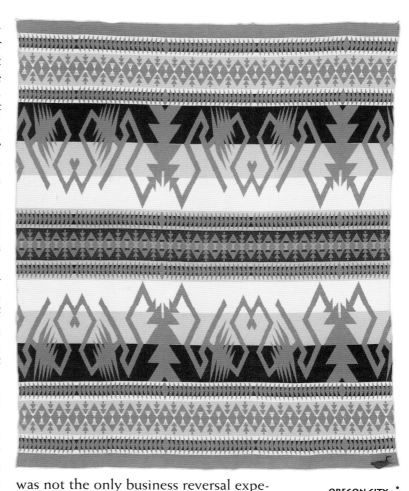

was not the only business reversal experienced by the brothers—the Oregon City mill was also heavily damaged by a flood in 1890.) The two had emigrated to the United States from Poland (one account says they were Russian) and made their way to San Francisco in 1854 when Ralph was twenty and Isaac was eighteen. The next year, they started business in Portland, with one brother peddling from a horse-drawn wagon in the Portland area while the other worked in the store they operated. A local merchant named Sol Marx advanced $1,000 to the ambitious brothers, and their business expanded.

OREGON CITY BANDED ROBE, FEATURED IN 1911 CATALOG.

JULIAN AND MARIA MARTINEZ WITH SON JOHN, SAN ILDEFONSO PUEBLO, 1926. JULIAN IS WEARING AN OREGON CITY BLANKET. (PHOTO BY ELIZABETH WILLIS DEHUFF, COURTESY MUSEUM OF NEW MEXICO, NEG. 26335)

They were both involved in the Oregon City mill from its early years. Ralph Jacobs had one son, Adolph, who became active in the family business, as did Isaac's three sons.

Because it dated back to 1864, Oregon City was one of the older of the major manufacturers of American Indian trade blankets. The company opened its first agency in New York in the early 1890s and, during its heyday, Oregon City was a major competitor with Pendleton Woolen Mills—the two firms struggled to dominate the Indian blanket trade. Following World War I, when Racine Woolen Mills, Buell Manufacturing Company, and J. Capps and Sons were no longer manufacturing trade blankets, Oregon City played a major role in the marketplace. Over the six decades Oregon City Woolen Mills was in operation, the company produced at least fifty different blanket designs—second only to Pendleton—and held onto a significant share of the trade blanket market into the Depression years, before it fell victim to the cash drought of the 1930s.

Oregon City Woolen Mills was a company very much in tune with the traditions of the Indian trade. The company's building near the Willamette River falls was erected on the site where Lewis and Clark first saw the falls of the Willamette River and where the Hudson's Bay Company erected a stockade.

And the company's promotional literature embellished this history whenever possible. The 1914 catalog stated, "In supplying these Blankets, we have naturally reproduced the Indian's most cherished patterns. Our designers are men steeped in Indian lore. They have worked side by side with the Indian and come into possession of his favorite designs and colorings, along with their symbolism."

OREGON CITY
BANDED ROBE.

Oregon City's executives made some shrewd business decisions in marketing "The Blanket of a 1000 Uses," even attaching a unique label to blankets intended for the Southwestern

Jacobs Oregon City Woolens

PURE VIRGIN WOOL — WOVEN WHERE THE WOOL IS GROWN

Indian Blankets

of fine quality
and unusual beauty

The desire for antiques, when garrets are ransacked for ancient treasures, has become popular again and has had its effect on increasing the demand for Indian blankets. For, while the blankets themselves are not antiques (being woven on modern looms), the designs were conceived by the Indians in the early days.

To the Indian his blankets were human documents. Into them he wove all his ambitions, hopes, his religious beliefs. And Oregon City blankets retain all the pathos and beauty of these designs.

X 1902-8

The red blanket pictured on the left is a big favorite. Red is a sacred color to the Indian, and blankets with red backgrounds were the choicest in his collection. Red meant sunshine—and sunshine was his life. Small wonder that he used it so abundantly in his blankets. Colors were used to convey ideas of locality and time, as well as myths of origin and romance.

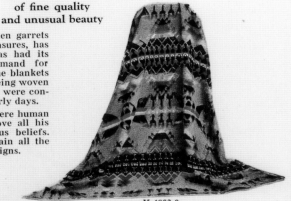

X 1918-42

The blankets shown on this page are our very best quality. They are woven from fine Merino wool. The fact that they are used extensively by the Navajo Indians themselves throughout Arizona and New Mexico, as well as other western tribes, is a fine tribute to their authentic designs, beautiful colors and high quality.

X 1900-66

—Prices and detailed description in back of catalogue

12

Indian trade through the C. N. Cotton Company. Oregon City also established a chain of retail stores in the West and Midwest and promoted the image of the company by entering and winning awards at major national and international exhibitions, including a first prize at the 1876 Philadelphia Centennial Exposition and a grand prize with seven gold medals from the Panama-Pacific International Exposition. This attention to detail even went so far as calling its model numbers "range" numbers, a more picturesque term that no doubt helped distinguish the Oregon City robes in the minds of retail and wholesale companies.

In 1919, the company initiated a series of full-page color advertisements in the *Saturday Evening Post*. The ads attracted attention for both the wholesale trade and the company's retail operations in Denver, Minneapolis, Oakland, San Francisco, Portland, Tacoma, and Oregon City. The company's retail stores prospered until the late 1920s, when the beginning of the Depression caused the chain to shrink to four locations—Seattle, Portland, San Francisco, and Tacoma.

The company told a romantic story of itself and its product:

Closely interwoven with the history of Oregon is the history of the Indian—his onslaughts, his brave battles, his retreat, and in the end the pitiful vanquishment of a noble race. To the Indian, everything is symbolic. The brilliant, resplendent colors so dear to his heart are an expression of his interpretations of Life—the green of the earth, the blue of the heavens, the flight of a flock of birds, the sweep of the winds and the splash of the waves. We are preserving the rare charm of Indian weaving by modern methods. All the beauty and significance originally woven into fabric by the Indian, on his crude hand loom, are retained in our perfectly woven Navajo Art-Craft fabrics.

FOR THE COLLECTOR OF OREGON CITY BLANKETS

I. SIZES AND WEIGHT:

From the 1914 catalog:

    Style x1242-40 measured 60″ x 70″, with felt-bound ends

    Style x1900-66 measured 62″ x 80″, with felt-bound ends

From the 1922 catalog:

    The blankets measured either 60″ x 76″ or 62″ x 80″ and were felt-bound. Bedspreads, also in the Indian blanket designs, measured 66″ x 80″ and were silk-bound. Less expensive Indian design blankets with whipped edges measured 60″ x 74″. The less expensive Hudson's Bay blankets had a whipped binding while the more expensive ones were bound in satin. They measured 66″ x 84″ and weighed 5 pounds.

II. NOTES ON CONSTRUCTION OF OREGON CITY WEAVINGS:

    Oregon City blankets were 80% to 85% wool weft, woven on a cotton warp.

    Oregon City's blankets are characterized by more intricate designs and more complex color combinations than the blankets produced by other mills. Unlike Pendleton, which always offered the fringed shawl or robe option as standard choice for its customers, Oregon City offered fringing only at an extra cost.

    Motor and steamer robes were finished with fringed ends.

III. LABELS:

    Most mills attached the label to the patternization side of the blanket. In contrast, Oregon City attached the label to the colorization side of its blankets. On the colorization side, the pattern is less distinct and is dominated by the colors of the blanket.

1″ X 1″
FIRST OREGON CITY LABEL, C. 1900.

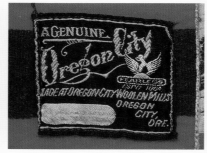

2 1/8″ X 1 3/4″
SECOND OREGON CITY LABEL, C. 1911–19. WHITE AREA IN THE LEFT-HAND CORNER HAD THE MANUFACTURERS' NAMES IN LIGHT INK, "J. TR JACOBS."

2 1/8″ X 1 3/4″
THIRD OREGON CITY LABEL, 1919–20. SCRIPT FOR "OREGON CITY" WAS DIFFERENT, APPEARED TYPESET.

2 1/8" X 1 3/4"
FOURTH OREGON CITY LABEL, 1920.
STARTING IN 1919, OREGON CITY CHANGED
THEIR LABEL TO READ "JACOB'S OREGON
CITY."

2 1/8" X 1 3/4"
FIFTH OREGON CITY LABEL, POST-1920. "A
GENUINE JACOB'S OREGON CITY."

Oregon City Woolen Mills produced three different label designs between 1919 and 1921.

One of the interesting labels produced by Oregon City Woolen Mills was the one attached to the blankets sent to C. N. Cotton Company, the southwestern regional wholesaler headquartered in Gallup, New Mexico. The label read:

> A Genuine Oregon City Robe
> Made Expressly for C. N. Cotton Co.
> Gallup, NM

The banner in the Oregon City label reads "Fearless," and this was a part of each of the different logo designs in Oregon City labels.

IV. BINDING OF THE OREGON CITY TRADE BLANKETS:

A whipstitched border was added to the less expensive Oregon City blankets. The edges of the higher-quality, more costly Oregon City blankets were bound with felt.

WHIPSTITCH BINDINGS WERE PLACED ON
OREGON CITY'S LESS EXPENSIVE BLANKETS.

FELT BINDINGS WERE USED ON OREGON
CITY'S MORE EXPENSIVE BLANKETS.

V. SPECIFICS ABOUT COLLECTING OREGON CITY BLANKETS:

Interesting novelty designs, including the Happy Hunting Ground design, the Totem Pole design, and special blankets for the Shrine Temple and the Elks Lodge.

◄ OREGON CITY OVERALL/BANDED "SWASTIKA" ROBE, FEATURED IN 1914 CATALOG.

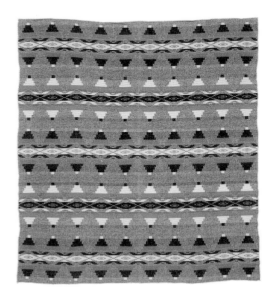

OREGON CITY BANDED ROBE. THIS PATTERN WAS OFFERED FOR TWENTY YEARS (1911–30s) AND WAS ONE OF THE MOST POPULAR. ►

OREGON CITY BANDED ROBE, FEATURED IN 1926 CATALOG. ◄

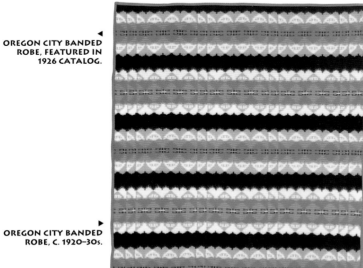

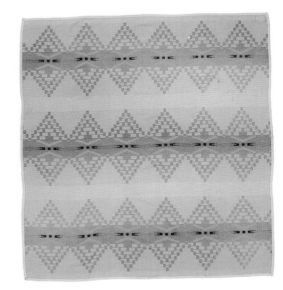

OREGON CITY BANDED ROBE, C. 1920–30s. ►

OREGON CITY NINE
ELEMENT ROBE,
FEATURED IN
1925 CATALOG.

OREGON CITY BANDED
ROBE, FEATURED IN
1923 CATALOG.

OREGON CITY CENTER
POINT SHAWL. THIS
BLANKET IS UNIQUE IN
THAT THE LABEL WAS
"MADE BY OREGON CITY
EXPRESSLY FOR C. N.
COTTON, GALLUP, N.M."

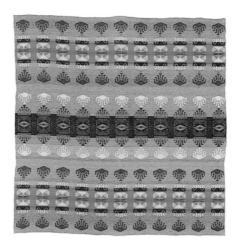

◀
OREGON CITY OVERALL ROBE, OFFERED FOR OVER TWENTY YEARS (1911–30s.)

▶
OREGON CITY OVERALL (BANDED) ROBE, FEATURED IN 1922–31 CATALOGS.

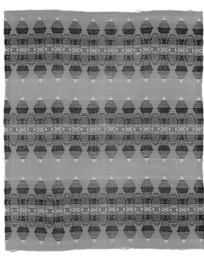

◀
OREGON CITY OVERALL (BANDED) ROBE, OFFERED FOR OVER TWENTY YEARS (1914–30s).

▶
OREGON CITY BANDED ROBE, C. 1920–30.

◀
OREGON CITY CENTER POINT (BANDED) ROBE, C. 1920s–30s.

▶
OREGON CITY CENTER POINT (BANDED) ROBE, FEATURED IN 1922–30 CATALOGS.

OREGON CITY BANDED
ROBE, FEATURED IN
1911 CATALOG.

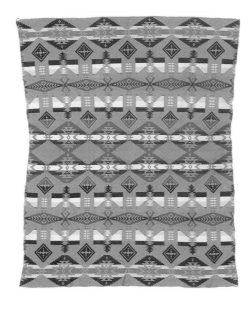

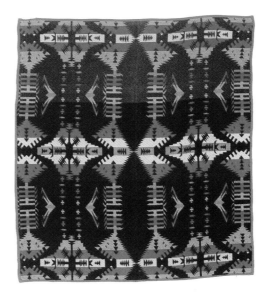

◄
**OREGON CITY BANDED
ROBE, FEATURED IN
1911 CATALOG.**

▶
**OREGON CITY CENTER
POINT ROBE, FEATURED
IN 1914 CATALOG.**

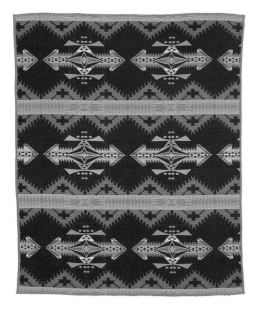

◄
**OREGON CITY SIX
ELEMENT ROBE,
C. 1920s–30s.**

▶
**OREGON CITY SIX
ELEMENT ROBE,
C. 1911–19 LABEL.**

BUELL THREE-COLOR ROBE WITH CLASSIC NAVAJO GEOMETRIC
DESIGN AND SPIDER FIGURE.

BUELL MANUFACTURING COMPANY

"THE ORIGINAL POWER LOOM MANUFACTURERS OF INDIAN ROBES"

THE BUELL MANUFACTURING COMPANY GREW FROM THE INDUSTRIOUS PIONEER ATTITUDE THAT WAS PREVALENT AMONG AMBITIOUS BUSINESSMEN OF THE MID-1800S. NORMAN BUELL TRAVELED FROM JEFFERSON COUNTY, NEW YORK, TO ILLINOIS WHERE HE OWNED A FIRM THAT MANUFACTURED WOOLENS. HIS SON, GEORGE, LEARNED THE INS AND OUTS OF WOOLEN MANUFACTURING IN THE FAMILY BUSINESS. SOON AFTER THE FAMILY MOVED TO ST. JOSEPH, MISSOURI, IN 1848, GEORGE W. BUELL MADE A DEPARTURE FROM THE FAMILY BUSINESS AND STARTED A SMALL SAWMILL. THIS ADVENTURE WAS FOLLOWED BY THE ESTABLISHMENT OF A FLOUR MILL IN WESTON, MISSOURI, IN THE NEXT COUNTY TO THE SOUTH OF ST. JOSEPH. IN ABOUT 1860, GEORGE BUELL RETURNED TO ST. JOSEPH AND TO THE SITE OF HIS SAWMILL, WHERE HE STARTED THE WOOLEN MILL THAT ULTIMATELY GREW INTO THE BUELL MANUFACTURING COMPANY. • BETWEEN 1860 AND 1867, GEORGE BUELL'S MILL WAS CALLED THE BUCHANAN WOOLEN MILL, NAMED FOR THE COUNTY IN WHICH IT WAS SITUATED. IT WAS PROSPEROUS FROM THE BEGINNING (HE SHOWED PROFITS RANGING FROM $11,000 TO $29,000 EACH YEAR), BUT IT WAS NOT UNTIL 1877 THAT A GROUP OF PARTNERS CAME TOGETHER TO FORM THE BUELL MANUFACTURING COMPANY. GEORGE BUELL WAS NAMED PRESIDENT OF THE FIRM AND REMAINED IN THAT OFFICE UNTIL HIS DEATH IN

1900. Under his direction, the mill grew steadily and expanded into the manufacture of blankets. One of the investors also owned a woolen mill in Blue Rapids, Kansas. Buell promotional materials explain that its blankets were made by more than one mill, so it is possible that some of the company's

George Buell and Company was listed as a company that manufactured only "Cassimeres and Yarns. 4 sets cards." Ten years later, Dockham's 1884 directory described the Buell Manu-facturing Company as a company that manufactured and sold "blankets, cassimeres and flannels, 10 sets cards, 65

COVER OF BUELL MANUFACTURING COMPANY CATALOG, C. 1912.

BUELL'S STYLE NUMBERS AND PREDOMINATING COLORS FROM THEIR 1912 CATALOG.

BUELL MFG. CO.=INDIAN ROBES
Style Numbers and Predominating Colors.

SIOUX			
0	X	XXX	
251	256		Red, Green, Yellow
252	257		Black, Yellow, Green (see cut)
253	258		Bronze, Red, Yellow
254	259		Yellow, Red, Green
MOHAWK			
261	266	271	Green
262	267	272	Red (see cut)
263	268	273	Purple
264	269	274	Magenta
OTOE			
281	286	291	Red, Yellow, White, Blue (see cut)
282	287	292	Bronze, Brown, Yellow, Vic.
283	288	293	Green, Red, White, Black
284	289	294	Red, Green, Yellow, Purple
MOKI			
301	306		Red, Green, Yellow
302	307		Magenta, Yellow, Green (see cut)
303	308		Red, White, Black
304	309		Blue, Yellow, White
ZUNI			
316	321		Red, Green, Yellow
317	322		Yellow, Red, Green (see cut)
318	323		Magenta, Red, Green
319	324		Bronze, Vic., Cream
HANOLCHADI			
331	336		Red, White, Black (see cut)
332	337		Yellow, White, Green, Red
333	338		Red, Green, Yellow
334	339		Brown, Bronze, Red
AZTEC			
	346		White, Red, Black, Green (see cut)
	347		Red, Black, White
	348		Green, Red, Black, Yellow
	349		Brown, Yellow, Green, Red
CHEYENNE			
	356		Black, Red, White
	357		Vic. Brown, Bronze
	358		Red, Black, Green
	359		Yellow, Green, Red (see cut)
SHOSHONI			
	366		Black, White, Red (see cut)
	367		Black, White, Yellow
	368		White, Red, Green
	369		Yellow, Brown, Red
CHEROKEE			
	376		Tan
	377		Light Blue
	378		Green (see cut)
	379		Red
COMANCHE			
	386		Red, Yellow, Green (see cut)
	387		Green, Gray, Red
	388		Old Rose, Blue, Green
	389		Light Blue, Pink, Tan

products were actually produced in the second mill, located in Kansas.

The Buell Manufacturing Company, with annual revenues of $250,000, was similar in size to other competing trade blanket manufacturing firms like J. Capps and Sons. In the 1874 *United States Textile Manufacturers' Directory*,

looms, steam power." Subsequent listings in 1891–92 and 1904–05 added new specialty items to the product line but pointed out that the company had fewer looms and sets of cards.

The 1904–05 World's Fair edition of *The Blue Book Textile Directory* listed Buell as manufacturing "Blankets, Indian and

Carriage Robes, 8 sets Cards. 57 Broad Looms." The firm's capitalization was $200,000 and it employed 175 people—very close in size to J. Capps and Sons at the same time. Buell Manufacturing Company was no longer listed in the St. Joseph, Missouri, telephone directory by 1912, so it apparently went out of business between the time of the 1905 *Textile Directory* listing and the publication of the 1912 *St. Joseph Telephone Directory*.

There is only one known catalog for the Buell Manufacturing Company's line of American Indian trade blankets, but there is another catalog produced by dry-goods distributor Tootle and Campbell for the years 1909–10. This catalog included twelve designs of Buell's Indian trade blankets, including the simple Idaho design. As was typical of the trade blanket advertising by all the companies marketing blankets early in the twentieth century, Buell focused on the non-Indian American's romantic notion of the American Indian.

In its catalog, Buell touted itself as "The Original Power Loom Manufacturers of Indian Robes" and its product as the best-made blankets in the country. Another marketing edge that Buell claimed was that, while other companies could only produce two-color blankets, it was producing three-color blankets—the only ones on the market. This claim applied to Buell's Cheyenne and Shoshoni design blankets.

And the two three-color blankets Buell produced are unique in the market. In most weaving on a Jacquard power loom, each horizontal line in the blanket can have only two colors. In any spot where one color disappears,

the other color must appear. This limitation does not apply to the vertical hand loom, like the ones used by Navajo weavers, who can use as many colors of yarn in each line as they please. All they need to do is set the color aside until they're ready to use it again.

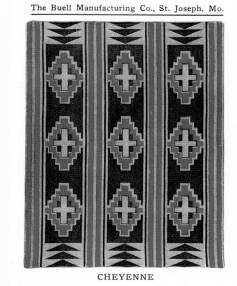

The Buell Manufacturing Co., St. Joseph, Mo.

CHEYENNE

In presenting this robe we wish to call your attention to the fact that this is the first time a mill has ever offered a three-color Indian robe **with a perfect design on both sides.** In order to accomplish this it has been found necessary to increase the weight of the robe materially, which of course adds to the cost. Made in four styles and one size only.

X—60x72 in.

11

BUELL CHEYENNE PATTERN.

Buell developed a technique of using three colors on one line by "hiding" the third color of yarn between the other two colors. The result is a unique design and a heavier blanket. One of these blankets can be seen in a striking photograph by William J. Boag of Peter Big Heart, chief of the Osage tribe, made in Pawhuska, Oklahoma, on August 23, 1909. In the photograph, Big Heart is wearing a Buell "Cherokee" design blanket—one of the three-color designs. Along with his blanket, Peter Big Heart is wearing beaded moccasins and a swastika pin on his vest as he holds a feather fan.

In romanticizing the blanket designs, the Buell catalog contains some misinformation. For example, one

◄
OSAGE CHIEF
PETER BIG HEART
IS WEARING A BUELL
"CHEROKEE" BLANKET.

►
BUELL NINE ELEMENT
"CHEYENNE" BLANKET.
THIS IS ONE OF
THE THREE-COLOR
BLANKETS BUELL
PRODUCED. UNLIKE THE
STANDARD
TWO COLORS OF
YARN PER LINE, THIS
HAS THREE COLORS.

banded blanket design that bears a resemblance to a historic Hopi manta is called "Zuni" in the catalog, and is described as a very close reproduction of the old Hopi ceremonial robe, this robe having been used in the cere-

monies of the Hopi or Moki tribe at their town of Zuñi for many years.

To anyone with even the most basic knowledge of the Southwestern Indians, this passage is ridiculous. Obviously, the Hopi villages found in Arizona are not part of the Zuñi pueblo. They live in the Hopi villages. But apparently, the company's advertising copywriters didn't know the difference between Hopi and Zuñi and

assumed that the non-Indian customers didn't know the difference either. This is simply an example of the kind of association that American Indian names had for advertising in the United States at the turn of the twentieth century.

Another example of this association is the pattern called the "Shoshoni," a distinctively Navajo weaving design. There is no real reason the company couldn't have assigned a Navajo name to the design except that perhaps "Shoshoni" sounded more poetic to someone in the advertising department. Another interesting piece of marketing misinformation goes along with the design called "Hanolchadi", a Third Phase Navajo Chief's blanket design. The Buell catalog states, "Hanolchadi, or Navajo Chiefs' blanket, is taken from an old design which was intended only for the chiefs and until recently held sacred to their use." Even if the names chosen for the company's blanket designs were not accurate, the Buell designs tended to have a more direct relationship with Native American weaving designs than did most of the blankets of other companies.

FOR THE COLLECTOR OF BUELL BLANKETS

I. SIZES AND WEIGHT:

Most designs for Buell blankets were produced in three sizes and four color combinations.
    Style O measured 50" x 68" and weighed 2 3/4 pounds.
    Style X measured 60" x 72" and weighed 3 pounds.
    Style XXX measured 64" x 80" and weighed 3 1/4 pounds.
    The Idaho design, a variation on the earlier blanket designs woven for the fur trade, was a one-color blanket with stripes at either end and the short "point" stripes woven into the pattern. For a more detailed explanation of the point blanket, see chapter three. This blanket measured 54" x 74" and was available in two weights—4 3/4 pounds or 5 3/4 pounds.

II. BINDING OF THE BUELL TRADE BLANKETS:

Close-up photograph with details. Buell blankets did not have a trade cloth binding. Buell blankets had a tight whipstitching that created a binding edge that measures approximately 1/4". A looser diagonal whipstitch about 3/8" long was then added over this tighter border binding.

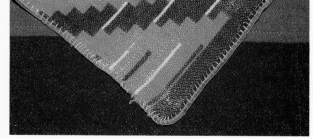

BUELL BLANKET SHOWING STITCHED BINDING.

III. SPECIFIC NOTES ABOUT COLLECTING BUELL BLANKETS:

Buell was the only one of the major trade blanket manufacturers to produce three-color blankets. These blankets—known as the "Cheyenne" and "Shoshoni" designs—were heavier than most trade blankets because each horizontal line included three colors of yarn rather than two. Buell developed a method of weaving the third color yarn between the other two colors, thus hiding it.
    Also, Buell marketed three trade blankets with designs based directly on earlier traditional Native American weaving styles. These were "Hanolchadi," a Third Phase Chief's blanket design; "Zuni," a striped Hopi manta design; and "Shoshoni," based on a regional Navajo weaving style.

230

DEPT. A.

TOOTLE·CAMPBELL DRY GOODS CO.

Buell's Indian Robes.

AZTEC.
Cut shows No. 346.
See page 231 for description.

CHEYENNE.
Cut shows No. 359.
See page 231 for description.

SHOSHONI.
Cut shows No. 366.
See page 231 for description.

CHEROKEE.
Cut shows No. 378.
See page 231 for description.

COMANCHE.
Cut shows No. 386.
See page 231 for description.

IDAHO BLANKETS.
Cut shows style of Nos. 500 and 600.
See page 231 for description.

PAGE FROM THE 1909–10 CATALOG OF TOOTLE-CAMPBELL DRY GOODS COMPANY, ST. JOSEPH, MO, ILLUSTRATING SIX STYLES OF BUELL BLANKETS.

▲
AHBAH KACHINA
MANTA BLANKET-
MAKER, HOPI, AZ,
C. 1902. THE BUELL
MANUFACTURING
COMPANY CREATED THE
"ZUNI" BLANKET BASED
ON THIS DESIGN.
(PHOTO BY ADAM C.
VROMAN, COURTESY
MUSEUM OF NEW
MEXICO,
NEG. 2577)

▶
BUELL "ZUNI"
BLANKET.

▲
BUELL BANDED
"CHEROKEE" PATTERN.

▶
BUELL CENTER
PATTERN (THIRD PHASE
CHIEF'S STYLE) ROBE.
BUELL NAMED THIS
THE "HANOLCHADI"
BLANKET.

RACINE BANDED ROBE. THIS BLANKET IS ILLUSTRATED IN A RACINE
BLANKET FLYER C. 1912. (SEE PHOTO ON PAGE 116, LOWER LEFT.)

RACINE WOOLEN MILLS
BADGER STATE BRAND

"THE INDIAN'S INSTINCT HAS BECOME THE WHITE MAN'S REASONING CHOICE."

EVEN THOUGH RACINE WOOLEN MILLS WAS IN BUSINESS AND OWNED BY MEMBERS OF THE SAME FAMILY FOR NEARLY A CENTURY, THE COMPANY PRODUCED INDIAN TRADE BLANKETS IN ITS OWN MILLS FOR LESS THAN THIRTY YEARS. AFTER THE RACINE MILLS WERE CLOSED IN 1912 THE COMPANY CONTINUED IN BUSINESS FOR ALMOST ANOTHER HALF CENTURY, BUT CONTRACTED WITH OTHER MILLS TO PRODUCE THE SHAWLS AND WEARING BLANKETS THAT IT SOLD TO INDIAN TRADERS. IN 1952, COMPANY OWNER JOHN S. HART PASSED AWAY, ENDING A CAREER OF FORTY YEARS WITH THE FIRM THAT WAS FOUNDED BY HIS TWO GRANDFATHERS IN 1863. IN AN INTERVIEW WITH A NEWSPAPER REPORTER IN THE EARLY YEARS OF HIS ASSOCIATION WITH HIS FAMILY'S FIRM (ABOUT 1915), HART EXPLAINED THAT MORE THAN FORTY INDIAN TRIBES WERE REGULAR CUSTOMERS OF THE RACINE WOOLEN MILLS. THE ARTICLE STATES, "THE INDIAN'S LOVE FOR GAUDY COLORS AND LOOSE GARMENTS DESPITE ALL THE CIVILIZATION THAT THE WHITE MAN HAS FORCED UPON HIM, RETAINS FOR THE RACINE WOOLEN MILLS A VERY VALUABLE SOURCE OF INCOME." • THE STORY OF THE COMPANY'S INVOLVEMENT IN THE INDIAN BLANKET TRADE STARTS WITH A SELLING TRIP THROUGH THE WESTERN AND SOUTHWESTERN STATES BY SANDS M. HART, JOHN HART'S FATHER. ON THIS TRIP, DURING THE LATE 1880S, SANDS HART TOOK NOTICE OF THE

Indians of different tribes that chose to wear brightly colored trade blankets "instead of conventional clothing." Since Racine Woolen Mills had already made a name for itself throughout the West and Midwest with its Beaver State brand shawls, the company was perfectly positioned to take advantage of the demand from the American Indian people for more brightly colored trade

RACINE BADGER STATE FRAMED SHAWL. THIS BLANKET STYLE WAS ONE OF THE FIRST BLANKETS OFFERED BY RACINE. NUMEROUS VINTAGE PHOTOGRAPHS SHOW PLAINS INDIAN WOMEN WEARING THIS STYLE OF SHAWL.

blankets and fringed shawls. Not only did the company develop a line of wearing blankets and shawls for the Indian trade, but it also made "an annual style appeal through new designs and new colors made up to please the Indian buck." This move opened up markets for Racine Woolen Mills on Indian reservations in Wisconsin, Idaho, Utah, Washington, Oregon,

Oklahoma, Arizona, New Mexico, North Dakota, and South Dakota.

Because of Racine Woolen Mills' location, the company's shawls were popular among the tribes of the Northern Plains. Historic photographs show many women of the Plains tribes wrapped in the plaid, striped, and plain-colored shawls that must have been the product of the Racine Woolen Mills.

Records indicate that Lucius Blake and John S. Hart founded the original Blake and Company in 1863 and, in 1865, reorganized the firm as Racine Woolen Mills—Blake and Company. The *Racine Weekly Advocate* gave a glowing account of the firm's activities in its February 28, 1866, issue. In "one of the best buildings in the city," Racine Woolen Mills housed a total of thirteen looms. On the building's fourth floor, the company operated additional machinery for processing wool and preparing cloth. One notorious piece of equipment was called the "Picker." The newspaper account says the "'Picker' could as appropriately be called the 'incendiary,' as many woolen factories have been destroyed by fire originating from its mad pranks." It was perhaps one of the Picker's "mad pranks" that destroyed the Racine Woolen Mills building in 1877. After the original mill was destroyed in the 1877 fire, Blake and Hart incorporated the firm under the same name. So, the years 1863, 1865, and 1877 were all important years in the firm's evolution. Another important year in the history of the Racine Woolen Mills was 1893, the year of the Columbian World Exhibition, where a collection of the

Racine company's finest American Indian trade blankets received an award for quality in production and in design.

In the early years of the twentieth century, Racine Woolen Mills was prominent nationally. In 1905, in an attempt to expand its operations into the West, the company made a bid to purchase the then-troubled Pendleton Woolen Mills in Pendleton, Oregon, with a promise to significantly expand that factory's capacity. Had the negotiations resulted in a solid agreement, the history of the American Indian trade blanket would be dramatically different today. But the negotiations failed, and the Pendleton company was purchased in 1909 by the Bishop family, which still owns the operation today.

Because it was a major local employer and a source of local pride, Racine Woolen Mills received regular coverage in the local press. In a clipping from the late 1930s, one story applauded the firm for "the unique distinction" of remaining in business in the same location for over seventy-three years, dealing in blankets, "Navajo rugs and other Indian goods." This mention of Navajo rugs is typical of the misinformation that was associated with the Indian blanket trade in the newspapers of the time. There was no distinction made between the Navajo weavings created by Navajo weavers and the commercially woven Indian trade blankets.

When reading through the company's promotional literature, it's easy to see how some of the facts concerning the Indian blanket trade could become confused. In the company catalog published in about 1915 one reads,

Before we took up the manufacture of Indian blankets the Indians made their own, but being handicapped by the lack of machinery and proper raw materials, they were unable to produce the kind of article they desired. The colors made from wood and berries were not fast, nor could a great variety be produced. The Indian woman, with her crude machinery, could not spin the yarn very fine, hence her product was coarse and heavy, more suitable for rugs than for a blanket to be worn.

COVER OF THE 1912 CATALOG PRODUCED BY RACINE WOOLEN MANUFACTURING COMPANY.

This description of the American Indian weaver is applicable to the Navajo weaving tradition, but certainly most of the Indian people who bought Racine blankets, or any other trade blanket, came from tribes that had no weaving tradition. By the end of the nineteenth century, the weavings produced by Navajo women were heavier and more appropriate for rugs than blankets. Racine, like the other trade blanket manufacturers of the time, presented its promotional material as if there was no other blanket manufacturer in the business.

"When the 'Racine Blanket,' made

also more critical of the "Indian robes" produced by its competitors, and openly questioned the "authenticity" of other companies' products. Records explain that Racine company executives actually stated that the Indian

ILLUSTRATION FROM RACINE 1912 CATALOG. THE "COZY CORNER GIRL" ADVERTISEMENT WAS USED BY ALL THE MAJOR MANUFACTURERS OF BLANKETS AS AN INCENTIVE FOR NON-INDIAN SALES.

on the finest machinery, and of high-grade materials, appeared, the Red man was delighted. Here was an article which was at once of pleasing patterns, rich in an array of bright colors, soft and pliable. Immediately they ceased making the trade blankets themselves and eagerly adopted the 'Pale Faced' production which far exceeded their fondest hopes." Racine's literature was

trade blanket market was the creation of Racine Woolen Mills, a claim that was repeated by other mills of the time.

Regardless of who created the Indian trade blanket market, Racine produced no more trade blankets on its own mills after the operation was closed in 1912. After the mill equipment was sold, Sands Hart, the man who is given the credit for getting

Racine Woolen Mills into the Indian blanket trade, purchased the company's remaining assets and reorganized the company as The Racine Woolen Manufacturing Company. He brought his two sons, Harold H. Hart and John S. Hart, into the business and contin-

until 1961.

Racine Woolen Mills was one of the smaller of the major manufacturers of American Indian trade blankets. The 1904–05 *Blue Book Textile Directory of the United States and Canada* lists Racine Woolen Mills as having $100,000 in

CLASS Y. Weight, 3½ pounds. Size, 62 x 78.

11

CLASS O. Weight, 3½ pounds. Size, 62 x 74.
Other colors are purple No. 613; pink No. 616 and white No. 617.

9

ued in the Indian trade, contracting with other mills to produce the shawls and robes that he sold to traders. Even though the blankets and shawls sold by Racine were produced by other mills, the designs were those originally produced by Racine Woolen Mills. The company continued on a limited basis

capital, five sets of cards and twenty-eight broad looms. It had added a few looms since the 1890–91 *Dockham's American Report and Directory of the Textile Manufacture and Dry Goods Trade* described the company as possessing five sets of cards, twenty-two broad looms and one narrow loom. The 1884

TWO BLANKET
PATTERNS
ILLUSTRATED IN
RACINE'S 1912
CATALOG.

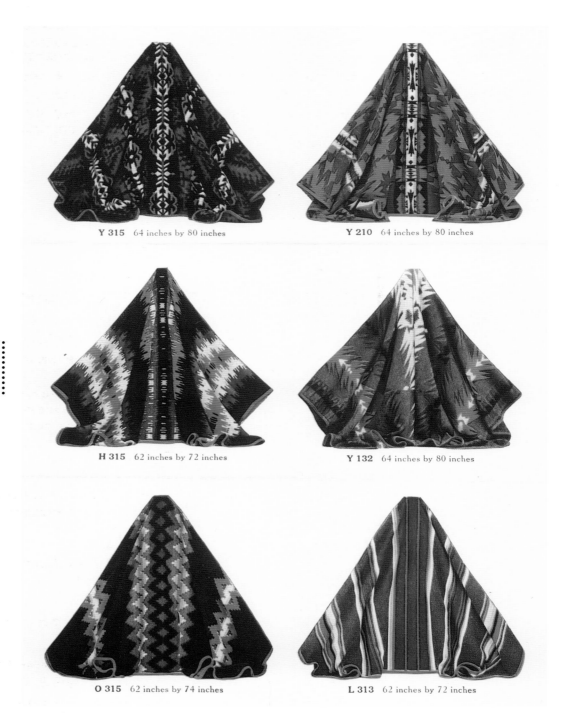

SIX EXAMPLES OF
RACINE BLANKETS
OFFERED IN SALES
FLYER C. 1912.

Y 315   64 inches by 80 inches

Y 210   64 inches by 80 inches

H 315   62 inches by 72 inches

Y 132   64 inches by 80 inches

O 315   62 inches by 74 inches

L 313   62 inches by 72 inches

Dockham's listed the same number of cards but only twenty looms. The 1874 *United States Textile Manufacturer's Directory* says Racine Woolen Mills had four sets of cards in its facility. This evidence explains that the company grew more slowly than some of its competitors during the same time.

Racine Woolen Mills was a success-ful manufacturing operation that might have become the largest trade blanket manufacturer in the country if its nego-tiations to purchase Pendleton Woolen Mills had succeeded. As the company's story turns out, Racine Woolen Mills made a stronger impact on its regional trade blanket market, particularly with its fringed shawls.

FOR THE COLLECTOR OF RACINE BLANKETS

I. SIZES AND WEIGHT:

The Racine Woolen Manufacturing Company's catalog that was published in about 1915 lists eight classes of trade blanket, each with slightly different weight and dimensions:

Class 175 measured 62" x 84" and weighed 5 pounds.

Class T measured 62" x 74" and weighed 4 1/2 pounds. The Class T was the only one of the eight blanket sizes that featured a smooth, sheared finish with no nap. All the other seven classes were "heavily napped," which means they were thicker and "fuzzier" and the designs were less distinct.

Class S measured 62" x 78" and weighed 3 3/4 pounds.

Class M measured 62" x 78" and weighed 3 1/2 pounds.

Class O measured 62" x 74" and weighed 3 1/4 pounds. Class O are the same size and weight as Class P blankets, but the Class O blankets are banded design blankets with geometric ele-ments, crosses and terraces within the bands.

Class Y weighed 3 1/4 pounds and measured 62" x 78".

Class P measured 62" x 74" and weighed 3 1/4 pounds. Class P blankets are the same weight and dimensions as the Class O blankets but are striped designs.

II. LABELS:

Several different paper labels were produced by Racine Woolen Mills. No labels were sewn onto the blankets, so they lack these identifying marks.

III. SPECIFIC NOTES ABOUT COLLECTING RACINE BLANKETS:

Fancy shawls were a characteristic product of the Racine Woolen Mills. These shawls were similar to trade blankets in design and construction but were almost always closer to square and were always fringed. Shawls were worn exclusively by Native American women.

COMANCHE WOMAN
AND CHILD WEARING
RACINE BLANKET. NOTE
THE TRADITIONAL
WAY TO CARRY A
CHILD WRAPPED IN
THE BLANKET.

RACINE
BANDED
SHAWL.

RACINE
BANDED
SHAWL.

RACINE BANDED
SHAWL, FEATURED IN
1912 CATALOG.

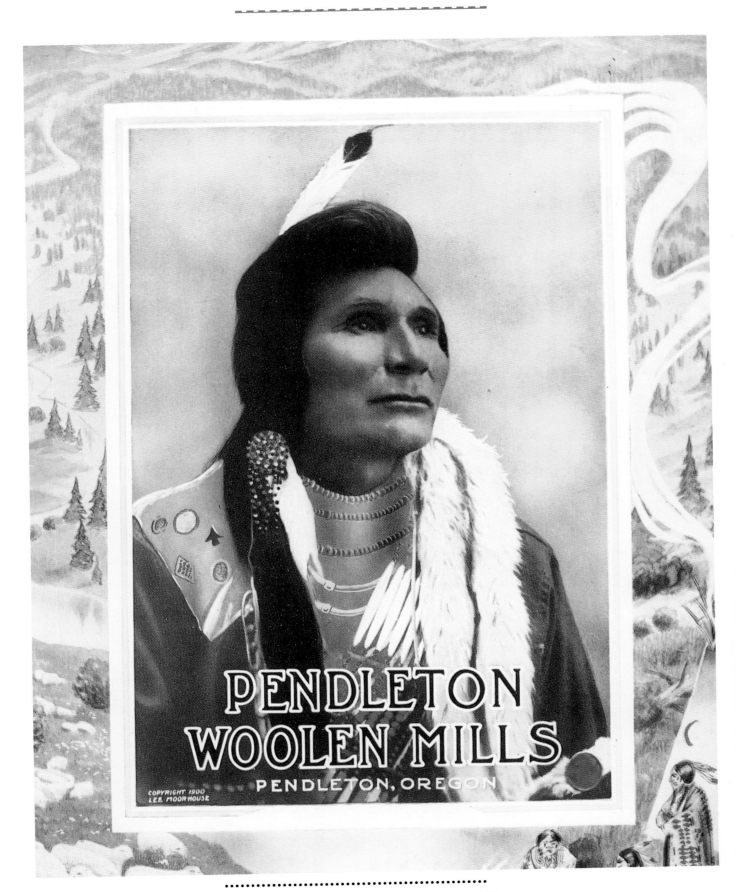

CATALOG COVER, 1910, PICTURES CHIEF UMAPINE. (THIS 32-PAGE
CATALOG WAS REPRINTED IN 1989 AND IS AVAILABLE FROM
AVANUYA PRESS IN ALBUQUERQUE, NM.)

CHAPTER ELEVEN

PENDLETON WOOLEN MILLS

GROUP OF VISITING BUSINESSMEN ON THE PENDLETON MILLS LOADING DOCK, 1910. C.M. BISHOP, OWNER, IS ON THE LEFT. (PHOTO BY W. S. BOWMAN, COURTESY UNIVERSITY OF OREGON LIBRARY.)

"THE MOST BEAUTIFUL AND POPULAR ROBE MADE."

PENDLETON IS UNDOUBTEDLY THE MOST RECOGNIZED NAME IN AMERICAN INDIAN TRADE BLANKETS. AND EVEN THOUGH THE ORIGINAL MILL WAS LOCATED IN OREGON, ITS NAME WAS SYNONYMOUS WITH QUALITY ACROSS THE UNITED STATES. WHEN C. N. COTTON ESTABLISHED HIS REGIONAL WHOLESALE BUSINESS, THE C. N. COTTON COMPANY IN GALLUP, NEW MEXICO, HE ILLUSTRATED HIS BUSINESS ACUMEN BY "OBTAINING EXCLUSIVE REGIONAL CONTROL OF TWO ITEMS BASIC TO THE NAVAJO TRADE: ARBUCKLE'S COFFEE AND PENDLETON BLANKETS. TO MOST NAVAJOS OF THAT TIME, ANY COFFEE OR BLANKET UNDER ANOTHER NAME WAS EITHER COUNTERFEIT OR AN INFERIOR SUBSTITUTE."[1] THIS SORT OF UNQUALIFIED ENDORSEMENT IS ONE OF THE REASONS THAT PENDLETON IS THE ONLY SURVIVING COMPANY THAT WAS ONE OF THE FIVE MAJOR MANUFACTURERS OF AMERICAN INDIAN TRADE BLANKETS IN THE EARLY 1900S. • BECAUSE THE WILLAMETTE VALLEY HAD DEVELOPED INTO A MAJOR WOOL-PRODUCING REGION, IT WAS ONLY NATURAL THAT INVESTORS from Europe and the eastern United States would pursue the establishment of a wool processing plant in Pendleton. By the late 1880s, specific plans for a wool scouring mill were discussed around town, and, by 1893, prominent local citizens, many of them members of the Pendleton Commercial Club, established the Pendleton Wool Scouring and Packing Company. Plant manager Theron Fell, an experienced rancher and wool-industry veteran, recognized that the town of Pendleton not only had all the necessary resources to support a successful wool processing operation, but it was also an ideal location for a woolen mill.

Fell's vision was based on the proven resources of the region. First, the area enjoyed an established reputation for producing high-quality wool. Second, the Umatilla River could supply both power to operate the plant and the substantial volume of water necessary for wool processing. And finally, there was a substantial experienced labor force to operate the mill.

In its first year of operation, the new plant proved that a wool scouring operation could be a success in Pendleton, as almost 4 million pounds of wool was processed. Fell continued to realize his plans to expand into production of finished woolen products. Even though raising adequate capital for such a venture was difficult, the ambitious Fell didn't wait for further proof; he developed a plan for the woolen mill idea and was among the six incorporators for Pendleton Woolen Mills in 1895. By mid-October 1896, the first batch of distinctive, round-cornered blankets produced by

the new Pendleton mill was ready for the market. As Christmas approached, the display room of the Pendleton Woolen Mills proudly exhibited the new blankets for the community to enjoy.

Because the early advertising for the mill was summarized in a placard that read "From the sheep's back to your back," it appeared that the primary business of the new mill would be the production of material for suits and clothing. However, from the beginning, Fell saw that the best market for the mill would be the nearby Umatilla Indian reservations and other reservations around the country.

Fell's decisions were based on marketing facts. At the time, the Indian population of the United States was estimated at nearly three hundred thousand with almost 50 percent of this number living in Indian Territory and in Navajo country of Arizona and New Mexico. Even in Oregon and the adjoining states of Washington and California, there were almost thirty thousand Indian people. To be sure that the Pendleton mills met the specific requirements of this diverse market, Fell dispatched a factory representative to visit reservations throughout the western United States. The goal was to weave "the correct designs and color demanded by the Indians of the different tribes." This research revealed that "robes with colors acceptable to the Crows in the North were unsalable to the Navajos in the Southwest."

Pendleton enlisted the help of Umatilla people from the nearby reservation to market the colorful blankets. The Umatilla modeled the robes and an illustrated brochure was made for the benefit of the traders and Indian agents around the country.

These marketing efforts paid off handsomely for Pendleton. In March 1897 Coffin Brothers, owners of three stores catering to the Indian populations of Lewiston, Lapwai, and Yakima, ordered a thousand blankets and stated that they expected to order fifteen hundred more to supply their market.[2]

The company produced its first catalog in about 1901. It was a small, three-by-five-inch brochure titled *The Story of the Wild Indian's Overcoat*. The cover featured the now-famous illustration of Chief Joseph, for whom one of the company's most famous designs is named, arrayed in a Pendleton Indian robe. Even though Chief Joseph is the most famous Indian leader associated with the Pendleton Mills, photographs of Umapine also appear on the company's promotional material, sometimes in a full-color portrait, and others (notably the 1927 catalog) in silhouette. In fact, the image of Umapine became something of a visual trademark for the Pendleton company.

Because the Pendleton mill was located so near the Umatilla Reservation, the company was readily able to develop its association with the American Indian people in its marketing efforts. The company made an effort to describe native traditions and customs in its advertising literature.

At the turn of the century, marketers were so eager to develop the romantic Indian theme for their customers that they created some images that are negative, particularly by today's standards.

One use of this Indian theme says:

This reservation [the Umatilla] is recognized not only as a social center, but as the emporium of Indian fashion. What a Paris hat is to a Chicago girl on Easter morning, a Pendleton robe is to the debutante of every reservation from Arizona to the Dakotas. The Umatilla buck is a fashion plate...

She [Mrs. Yellow Hawk] is a lady of judgment, she is willing to pay a good price for a Pendleton robe, knowing that it will be bright and serviceable long after the cheaper grades have been thrown aside for saddle blankets...

Our pale-face trade is not unlike that with the red man. We make robes in college colors; crimson and white, orange and black, crimson with navy blue, etc., each college town preparing its own colors.

Pendleton's aggressive marketing efforts continued through the early years of the twentieth century, with the company continuing to build an image on its association with the Indian people. Most of the promotional efforts included advertising, direct mail solicitation, and cards with color

The Story of the
Wild Indian's Overcoat

The Historic Chief Joseph of the Nez Perces

Arrayed in a Pendleton Indian Robe

COVER OF THE PENDLETON CATALOG, C. 1901. BESIDES BLANKETS, THIS 24-PAGE CATALOG OFFERED MOORHOUSE PHOTOGRAPHS OF PLATEAU INDIANS FOR SALE.

images of Indian people wearing Pendleton blankets.

During this time, the Pendleton Woolen Mills also developed a distinctive red trademark that consisted of three circles. In the larger center circle was an Indian woman, seated at a loom. In each of the two smaller circles (there was one on each side of the larger cir-

cle) there was a ram's head. Over the entire trademark was the slogan, "Pendleton Goods are Fleece Wool."

The original Pendleton Woolen Mills acquired its first Jacquard loom in July of 1901 and hired an Englishman named Joseph Rawnsley to operate it. Rawnsley had become acquainted with mill manager T. E. Fell's brother, George, at the Philadelphia Textile School, where both were learning about the latest loom technology. After they completed the course in Philadelphia, George Fell and Rawnsley traveled to Pendleton, and the job of developing Indian design blankets on the new loom fell to the Englishman. Rawnsley was to continue his association with Pendleton Mills under the ownership of the Bishop family until his death in 1929, and he became one of the most noted designers of Indian trade blankets.

Despite the Pendleton Woolen Mills' early successes, extensive marketing efforts, and far-reaching advertising, the business encountered hard times in the early 1900s. There was an insurmountable conflict between Theron Fell and E. Y. Judd regarding the direction the company should take. In fact, the conflict became so dramatic that Fell actually negotiated with the Oregon City Woolen Mill to fill some of Pendleton's orders. Through this process, Oregon City was able to develop a profitable relationship with C. N. Cotton in Gallup, New Mexico, one of the major distributors of American Indian trade blankets. This relationship gave Oregon City the incentive it needed to compete successfully with Pendleton.

Pendleton's operational problems continued to the point that, in 1905, the Racine Woolen Mills expressed an interest in purchasing the plant in order to expand its operations in the West. Although records are unclear about the reasons, these negotiations didn't bear fruit, and Pendleton's production dwindled over the next few years.

In 1909, a concerned Pendleton-area legislator approached an experienced wool industry figure, C. P. Bishop, with a plan to revive the ailing Pendleton Woolen Mills. Bishop's father-in-law was wool-industry pioneer Thomas Kay, so he and his sons, Clarence and Roy Bishop, all had extensive experience in the region's woolen mills. The Bishop family developed a plan to make a significant investment in the Pendleton Mills that would be matched by local investors. Clarence and Roy Bishop, both graduates of the Philadelphia Textile School, updated the factory and renewed the company's commitment to the Indian blanket trade. The Bishop family has maintained that commitment made in 1909 and still owns the Pendleton Woolen Mills.

In 1910, the company brought out its first illustrated color catalog under the new owners. The trade blanket designs incorporated American Indian design elements and patterns, and Pendleton named them "Indian pattern blankets" rather than "Indian blankets."

In the advertising literature produced for the company, the interaction between Pendleton and the Umatilla tribe was somewhat exaggerated. The catalog says, "The Indian could bring in his favorite designs and have them woven into a fleecy robe of gorgeous hue." This implies that each individual could commission a blanket, when the reality is that, even though several of the Pendleton designs were derived from traditional design elements, they were rarely commissioned by individuals.

The company produced three brands and quality grades: The top

CHIEF YELLOW HAWK AND MRS. YELLOW HAWK. CARDBOARD LABEL ATTACHED TO PENDLETON BLANKETS C. 1900–04.

grade was the all-wool Pendleton robe; the intermediate grade was the Beaver State blanket which was constructed using cotton warp; the lower-grade Cayuse blanket used 17 percent reprocessed wool. Collectors should note that, for one year only, Pendleton produced the less expensive Blackfoot brand blanket in three patterns.

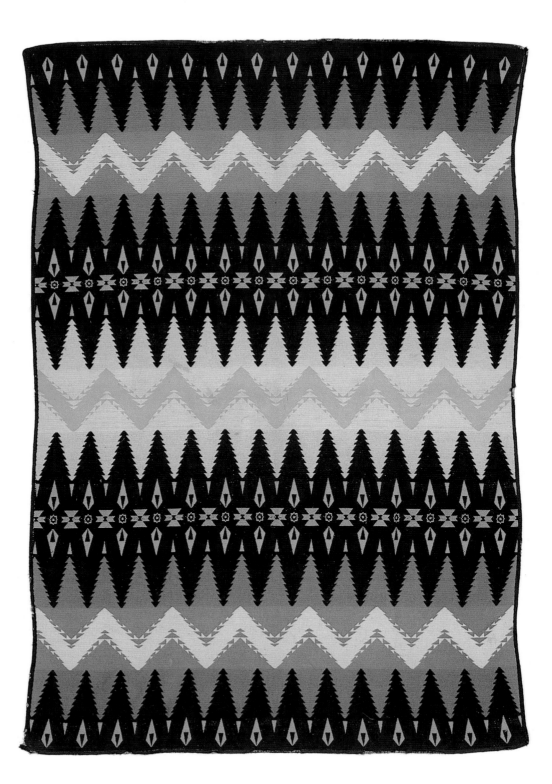

PENDLETON BANDED
ROBE, FIRST FEATURED
IN 1904 CATALOG
AND ALSO IN 1910
CATALOG.

Although some Pendleton designs were available in only one or two base colors, most patterns were available in as many as fifteen color combinations.

In its marketing, Pendleton continued the association with the Native American people, going so far as to say that "Pendleton originated the true Indian blanket." Pendleton developed a tradition of commemorative patterns named for specific individuals. One of the most famous is the Chief Joseph pattern, named for the Nez Perce leader. At the 1923 dedication of the Old Oregon Trail at Meacham, Oregon, Pendleton presented Mrs. Warren G. Harding with a commemorative blanket designed in her honor.

Because of quality production and design, Pendleton's Indian trade blankets became known as "the most distinctive blankets in America." Catalogs included full-color illustrations of many of Pendleton's most popular trade blanket designs, including "The Famous Harding" pattern with its distinctive white background and nine element design featuring three rows of three crosses. Another well-known Pendleton design popular at the time was the "Pendleton Tepee" pattern, a pattern which was produced in only a brown background. The Pendleton Tepee pattern is similar to a blanket design that was produced at about the same time by Oregon City Woolen Mills.

Even though Pendleton gave interesting names to some of its more distinctive patterns, most blankets were simply given model numbers. It is unfortunate for collectors in the 1990s that more blankets weren't given names because a name makes it much easier to

trace a particular blanket. One of the company's famous blankets, the "Glacier Park" blanket, is designed like the Hudson's Bay blanket. It is one of several Pendleton blanket designs named for national parks. The "Grand Canyon" blanket featured bands of narrow stripes at top and bottom against a

INDIAN ROBE. No. WT.

PRICE

MANUFACTURED BY THE PENDLETON WOOLEN MILLS PENDLETON, OREGON.

PEO, CHIEF OF UMATILLAS.

CHIEF PEO.
CARDBOARD
LABEL C. 1900–04.

black background, and the "Bryce Canyon" had colorful serape stripes. These three "National Park" blankets were distinctive; they were extremely plain compared to the other Pendleton designs, particularly the striking "Chief Joseph" pattern.

The descriptions of the blankets in catalogs of the twenties and thirties were vibrant. The "Chief Joseph" was characterized as "significant of this great chief's bravery and strength of personality—he commanded the respect and admiration of all during both peace and war. Truly Indian in design and color." The Nez Perce design "will remind you of the deep pine forests—with rays of sunlight peeping through. It's nature's handiwork at painting landscapes, forests and hills in green, red and yellow, with turquoise blue sky, that no doubt give

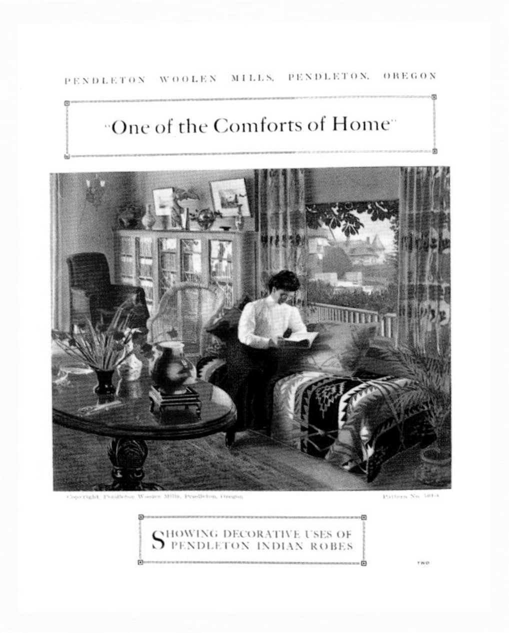

PENDLETON WOOLEN MILLS, PENDLETON, OREGON

·One of the Comforts of Home·

SHOWING DECORATIVE USES OF PENDLETON INDIAN ROBES

the Indian ideas for color and design."

Marketing information about the Tepee pattern blanket stated:

Indians buy many of these robes each year—and have ever since it was first made. It must remind them of their teepee homes among the green firs, with patches of snow here and there on the bleak, brown mountainside.

In order to market its Indian trade blankets to the American cowboy, Pendleton Mills offered its blankets through the Hamley Company, another firm located in Pendleton, Oregon, and one that marketed its products through catalogs. Saddles were the Hamley Company's stock in trade. Hamley Saddles, the 1919 catalog says, are "For Men Who Care." The Pendleton blankets offered in the Hamley catalog are the same blankets offered through the Pendleton Mills' general product catalog—"The 'Pendleton' Line of Pure Fleece Wool Products." There were apparently no special edition blankets designed for the Hamley Company.

In explaining the Pendleton Indian trade blankets, the Hamley 1919 catalog states, "'Pendleton' Indian Robes originated in the tepees of the wilderness. The wonderful designs and colorings of these robes are especially adapted for the adornment of our modern homes, greatly beautifying living room, cozy corner or den." Note that "new colors are being added to the line continually and old ones dropped."

In its 1928 catalog, one reads:

Listed on this page are the three types of Genuine Indian Blankets, made by the celebrated Pendleton Woolen Mills. These are not only used by the majority of Indian tribes throughout America, but by all red-blooded, out-door folk...

Hamley offered a good selection of Pendleton blankets for fifteen dollars, Beaver State blankets for seventeen to twenty dollars, and Cayuse blankets for ten dollars. Fringed shawls were available in each style for an additional charge that ranged from one to three dollars.

No doubt the Hamley's catalog was an effective way for Pendleton to reach the "cowboy" market, but the company also took aim at the western enthusiast through its sponsorship of the Pendleton Round-up, beginning with the 1913 event and continuing to the present. The company advertised in the Round-up program and was an enthusiastic sponsor of the annual rodeo that brought thousands of visitors to Pendleton every year. Even today, a traditional part of each winner's take is a red-and-black Pendleton Let 'Er Buck pictorial blanket.

By the late 1920s, Pendleton was a well-established company with an extensive product line that included all kinds of clothing in addition to the Indian trade blankets. It processed approximately three million pounds of wool produced in Oregon and the surrounding states of Idaho, Washington, and California. The company employed five hundred workers and achieved annual revenues of 3 million dollars. Because the Pendleton mill was occupied to capacity with the production of Indian trade blankets, the company took over additional mills in Washougal, Washington (formerly the Union Woolen Mills); Marysville, California (formerly the Marysville Woolen Mills); and Eureka, California (formerly the Humboldt Woolen Mills), for production of other woolen products.

Until World War II, the Pendleton Woolen Mills continued to produce Indian trade blankets in more than two hundred different patterns. After the war, the Pendleton trade blanket line changed drastically as the number of different patterns dropped to less than two dozen. In recent years, the company has added limited-edition commemorative blankets to its production. The generations-old Babbitt Brothers Trading Company has commissioned two different Navajo storm pattern blankets and the Hubbell Trading Post has commissioned a commemorative blanket designed like the classic

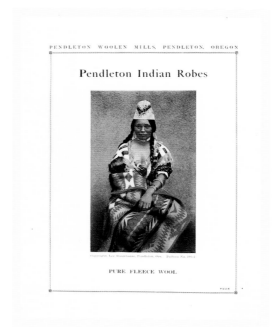

PENDLETON WOOLEN MILLS, PENDLETON, OREGON

Pendleton Indian Robes

PURE FLEECE WOOL

FOUR

UMATILLA WOMAN AND CHILD FROM PAGE FOUR OF 1910 CATALOG.

Navajo Third Phase Chief's blanket. Pendleton Woolen Mills still supplies the entire contemporary American Indian trade blanket market—and, because of increased interest, that market is expanding.

FOR THE COLLECTOR OF PENDLETON BLANKETS

I. SIZES AND WEIGHT:

Prior to the Bishop family's ownership, the Pendleton and Beaver State blankets produced by the Pendleton Woolen Mills weighed 3 to 3 1/4 pounds and measured 60" wide x 70" to 74" long (from 1925 catalog).

Blankets: 62" x 78"
Shawls: 64" x 78" (yarn-fringed)
Auto robe: 68" x 86" (felt-bound)
Couch cover: 60" x 108"

Cayuse Brand blankets
(felt-bound):
Blankets: 62" x 74"
Shawls: 64" x 64" (yarn-fringed)

II. NOTES ON CONSTRUCTION OF PENDLETON WEAVINGS:

The Pendleton brand blanket is all wool, both warp and weft.

The Beaver State brand, more common in trade blankets, is "pure fleece wool" filling on a cotton warp (as is the Cayuse brand). The nap is "shorn" on the Beaver State blankets so that the design is sharper.

III. LABELS:

There were four different Pendleton labels. Each blanket also came with a paper label.

History with photographs shows at least four distinct label styles.

FIRST LABEL USED ON PENDLETON BLANKETS, 1904, 2 1/8" X 1". "GUARANTEED TO BE A PENDLETON FROM PENDLETON, OREGON, PURE FLEECE WOOL." IT WAS FIRST ATTACHED ON THE LOWER LEFT-HAND SIDE OF BLANKETS FROM, 1904–10. FROM 1910 TO THE PRESENT, THE LABEL HAS BEEN ATTACHED ON THE LOWER RIGHT-HAND SIDE OF BLANKETS.

SECOND PENDLETON LABEL, C. 1915–20, 2 1/8" X 1". "WARRANTED TO BE A PENDLETON, PENDLETON WOOLEN MILLS, PENDLETON, OREGON."

THIRD PENDLETON LABEL, 1921–30, 2 3/8" X 1". "WARRANTED TO BE A PENDLETON, COPYRIGHT 1921 BY PENDLETON WOOLEN MILLS, PENDLETON, OREGON."

FOURTH PENDLETON LABEL, 1930s–41, 2 3/8" X 1". "WARRANTED TO BE A PENDLETON, TRADEMARK REG. U.S. PAT. OFF., PENDLETON WOOLEN MILLS, PENDLETON, OREGON."

FIRST BEAVER STATE LABEL, 1915–22, 2" X 1". "BEAVER STATE, MADE BY PENDLETON WOOLEN MILLS, PENDLETON, OREGON." "ROBES AND SHAWLS" UPPER RIGHT.

SECOND BEAVER STATE LABEL, 1923–30, 2 1/4" X 1". "BEAVER STATE, COPYRIGHTED 1923 BY PENDLETON WOOLEN MILLS, PENDLETON, OREGON." "ROBES AND SHAWLS" UPPER RIGHT.

THIRD BEAVER STATE LABEL, 1930–72, 2 3/8" X 1". "BEAVER STATE, REG. U.S. PAT. OFF., PENDLETON WOOLEN MILLS, PENDLETON, OREGON." "ROBES AND SHAWLS" UPPER RIGHT.

FOURTH BEAVER STATE LABEL, 1972–PRESENT, 2 1/4" X 1 1/4". "BEAVER STATE, REG. U.S. PAT. OFF., PENDLETON WOOLEN MILLS, PENDLETON, OREGON." "ROBES AND SHAWLS" UNDER PENDLETON, OREGON.

FIRST CAYUSE INDIAN BLANKET LABEL, 1915–21, 2 3/8" X 1". "CAYUSE INDIAN BLANKET, MANUFACTURED BY PENDLETON WOOLEN MILLS, PENDLETON, OREGON." NOTE: "MANUFACTURED" STARTS BELOW THE E IN CAYUSE.

SECOND CAYUSE INDIAN BLANKET LABEL, 1921–30, 2 1/4" X 1". NOTE: "MANUFACTURED" STARTS UNDER THE A IN CAYUSE.

THIRD CAYUSE INDIAN BLANKET LABEL, 1930–41, 2 3/8" X 1". "REG. U.S. PAT. OFF."

BLACKFOOT ROBE LABEL, C. 1924, 2 1/4" X 1".

In the 1904 catalog, the Pendleton blankets had round corners and the label was on the left-hand side.

The "Pure Fleece Wool" label was not in the 1903 catalog featuring round-cornered blankets.

After the Bishop family purchased Pendleton Woolen Mills in 1909, the label was moved from the left side to the right side. After 1910, each blanket was given a paper "pure fleece wool" label. All blankets had square corners after this time.

The 1921 copyrighted label states:

> WARRANTED TO BE A PENDLETON
> copyright 1921
> by Pendleton Woolen Mills
> Pendleton, Oregon

1971—The Warner Woven Label Company, which supplied labels for the Pendleton blankets, produced a batch of labels that was darker than the standard production labels—almost black and gold rather than blue and gold. Even though this caused some confusion about the labels, it also provides a convenient landmark to date the blankets.

IV. BINDING OF THE PENDLETON TRADE BLANKETS:

The early Pendleton blankets produced in the 1890s were bound with flannel, double-stitched with silk thread. All brands of early Pendleton blankets produced for the Anglo trade were bound with silk.

ROUND CORNER BLANKET BINDING.

TRADITIONAL FELT BINDING FOR ROBES IS STILL BEING USED TODAY.

Pendleton Indian Blankets and Shawls

The Indian's Choice and the White Man's, Too

THE INDIAN has never found a blanket comparable to Pendletons in quality, serviceability or with coloring and marking so genuinely expressive of his own inherent art. Thus, Pendletons have no rival in the Indian's estimation. And, likewise, the white man appreciates Pendletons for that same high quality, that serviceability which severest hardship in usage cannot lessen, and for the perpetuation of true Indian art which the blankets represent. The patterns in Pendleton Indian Blankets are numerous and their color combinations varied. See Color Plates on Page 10.

PENDLETONS supply colorful "atmosphere" when displayed in the windows with clothing or other paraphernalia for any outing—supplying their own sales appeal for comfort.

Pendleton Indian Blanket
Pattern No. 116, Color 16

Find Ready Sale the Year Round

EVERY season of the year carries its particular use for Pendleton Indian Blankets—when they may be attractively featured and find ready acceptance for motoring, canoeing, camping, picnicing, on the beaches and for all Winter sports. In the home, too, they have innumerable uses—as couch covers, throws, slumber robes, on the sleeping porches, on the verandas, etc. Then, there is their popularity with the young people at college—for use in the dormitories and for all outings.

Pendleton Indian Blanket
Pattern No. 27, Color 28

[4]

Pendleton - Virgin Wool

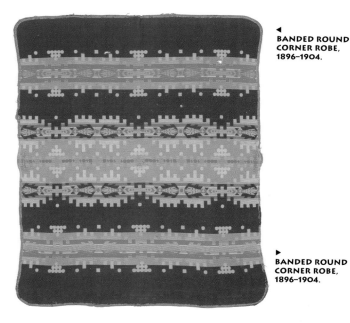

◀ BANDED ROUND
CORNER ROBE,
1896–1904.

▶ BANDED ROUND
CORNER ROBE,
1896–1904.

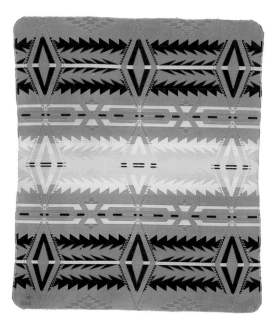

◀ OVERALL ROUND
CORNER ROBE,
1896–1904.

▶ NINE ELEMENT ROUND
CORNER, 1904–10. NOTE
THE REMNANT OF THE
LABEL IN THE LOWER
LEFT CORNER.

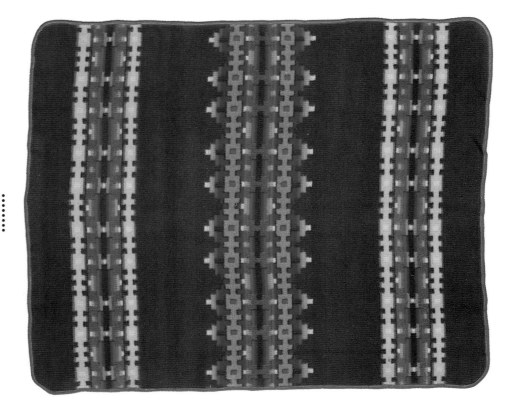

BANDED
ROUND CORNER,
C. 1896–1904.

RUTH COYOTE
AND CHILD. THIS
MOORHOUSE
PHOTOGRAPH,
C. 1900, ILLUSTRATES
A ROUND CORNER
PENDLETON.
(COURTESY
BOB KAPOUN)

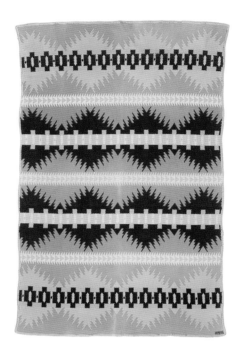

◄ BANDED SHAWL,
C. 1910 (HAS FIRST
PENDLETON LABEL—
PURE FLEECE WOOL).

► BANDED ROBE
(FEATURED IN 1904
AND 1910 CATALOGS).

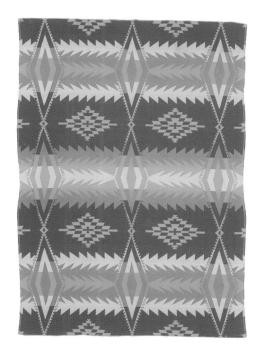

◄ NINE ELEMENT ROBE
(FIRST FEATURED IN
1904 CATALOG AS
ROUND CORNER, ALSO
IN 1910 AS SQUARE).

► OVERALL ROBE
(FEATURED AS ROUND
CORNER BLANKET IN
1904 CATALOG, AS
SQUARE BLANKET IN
1910 CATALOG).

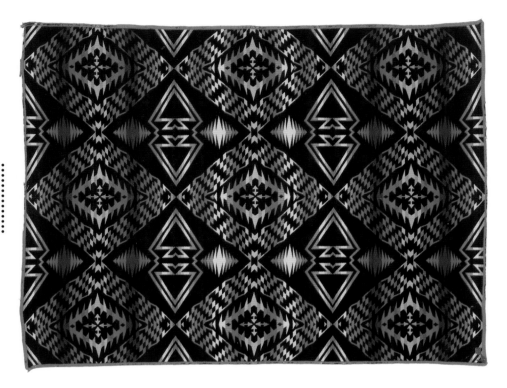

NINE ELEMENT ROBE.
THE DESIGN AND
COLOR COMBINATION
MAKE THIS BLANKET
AN "EYE DAZZLER."

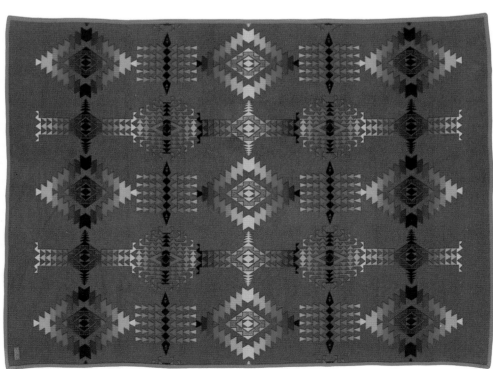

NINE ELEMENT
ROBE, PENDLETON
REG. LABEL. THIS
BLANKET WAS
FEATURED IN THE
1932 HAMLEY
COWBOY CATALOG
(PENDLETON,
OREGON) AS THE
"YAKIMA."

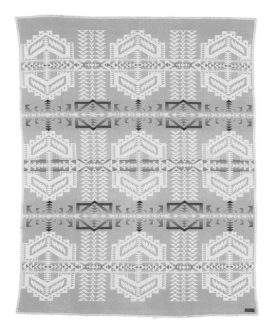

◀ **NINE ELEMENT ROBE,**
PENDLETON 1921 LABEL.

▶ **NINE ELEMENT ROBE,**
PENDLETON 1921 LABEL.

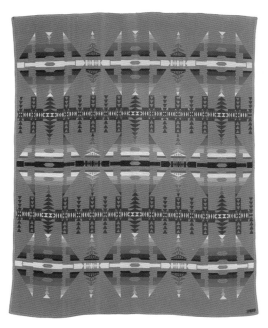

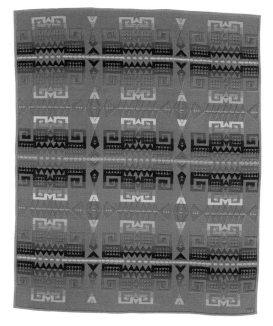

◀ **NINE ELEMENT ROBE,**
PENDLETON 1921 LABEL.

▶ **NINE ELEMENT ROBE,**
PENDLETON 1921 LABEL.

SUSANA AGUILAR,
SAN ILDEFONSO
PUEBLO, CA, 1925–30.
THIS BLANKET WAS
PRODUCED BY
PENDLETON AS EARLY
AS 1904. (PHOTO
BY T. HARMON
PARKHURST, COURTESY
MUSEUM OF NEW
MEXICO, NEG. 43755)

OVERALL ROBE, 1910 CATALOG.

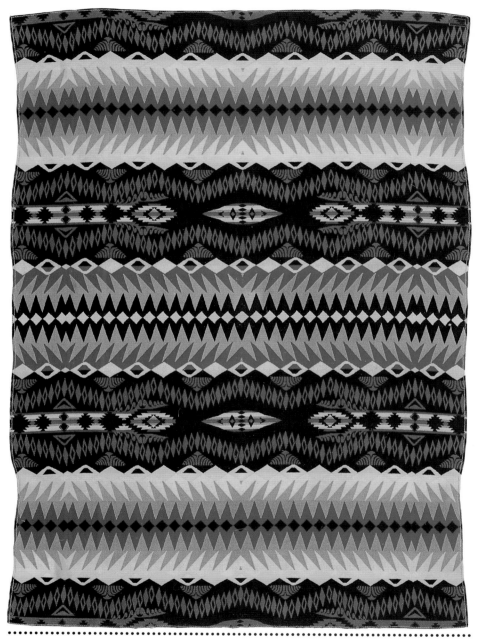

PLATEAU INDIAN
WOMAN PROUDLY
DISPLAYING HER
NEW PENDLETON
BLANKET, WITH
BOTH THE LABELS
STILL ATTACHED.
NOTE THE LARGE
PAPER LABEL ABOVE
THE "PURE FLEECE
WOOL" SILK LABEL.
(PHOTO COURTESY
OREGON HISTORICAL
SOCIETY)

BANDED ROBE, 1910 CATALOG (FEATURED IN THE 1904 CATALOG AS A ROUND CORNER BLANKET).

GERONIMO. THIS FAMOUS APACHE CHIEF WAS PHOTOGRAPHED WEARING A 1904–10 ROUND CORNER PENDLETON WITH THE LABEL QUITE VISIBLE IN THE LOWER LEFT CORNER OF THE BLANKET. (PHOTO COURTESY DENVER PUBLIC LIBRARY, WESTERN HISTORY DEPARTMENT)

Pendleton Beaver State Quality Robes and Shawls

No. 2800 Beaver State Robe
No. 1800 Beaver State Shawl
Color 9¾

Extra Quality Pendletons

ON THIS page and the two following are the "superlative" Pendletons, those known as "Beaver States". These blankets are larger and heavier than Pendletons — having more intricate patterns. The nap is shorn, leaving a soft, velvety effect and more distinct color definition. Thus, they command a higher price than Pendletons. Beaver State Robes and Shawls, as Pendletons, are made with Virgin Wool Filling on Cotton Warp. The various body colors for those pictured are shown in the Swatch Plates on Page 11. Order Blanket by number, and color as follows:

No. 0	—Red	No. 5	—Black
No. 1	—Blue	No. 6	—White
No. 1½	—Sapphire Blue	No. 7	—Pink
No. 2	—Green	No. 8	—Grey
No. 3	—Purple	No. 9	—Brown
No. 4	—Magenta	No. 9½	—Tan
		No. 9¾	—Drab

Of Historic Interest to Every Buyer

BEAVER STATE quality "Pendletons" were originally conceived for the Indian's exclusive use, and from their home in the heart of the great Cayuse and Umatilla Indian country the fame and usage of these fine Blankets spread to the other Indian tribes throughout America.

But these picturesque and serviceable "Beaver States" were not destined to remain forever the Indian's prized possession alone. They have captured the fancy of the red-blooded white man and woman, who find in them equally as wide a range of utility in their homes and for their outdoor adventures.

You as a dealer may couple this romantic history with the desirability of these Blankets and find a selling appeal that is rarely afforded in the handling of merchandise.

No. 2900 Beaver State Robe
No. 1900 Beaver State Shawl
Color 1½

[6]

Pendleton - Virgin Wool

BEAVER STATE BANDED
SHAWL, C. 1930s. ONE
EXAMPLE OF THE FEW
BLANKETS THAT USED
ONLY TWO COLORS.

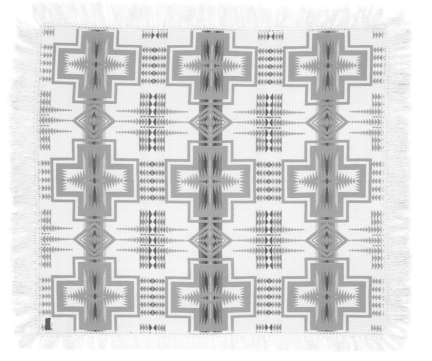

NINE ELEMENT
HARDING SHAWL,
COPYRIGHT 1923 LABEL.
THIS BLANKET IS STILL
IN PRODUCTION.

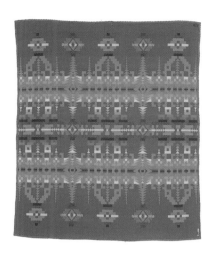

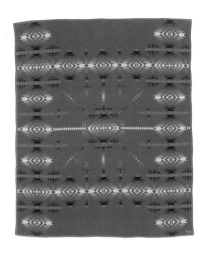

BEAVER STATE OVERALL
C. 1920–30s.

BEAVER STATE FRAMED
ROBE, COPYRIGHT 1923
LABEL.

BEAVER STATE BANDED
ROBE, C. 1920–30s.

BEAVER STATE BANDED
SHAWL, COPYRIGHT 1923
LABEL.

BEAVER STATE STRIPED
ROBE, COPYRIGHT 1923
LABEL.

BEAVER STATE
CENTER POINT ROBE,
COPYRIGHT 1923 LABEL.

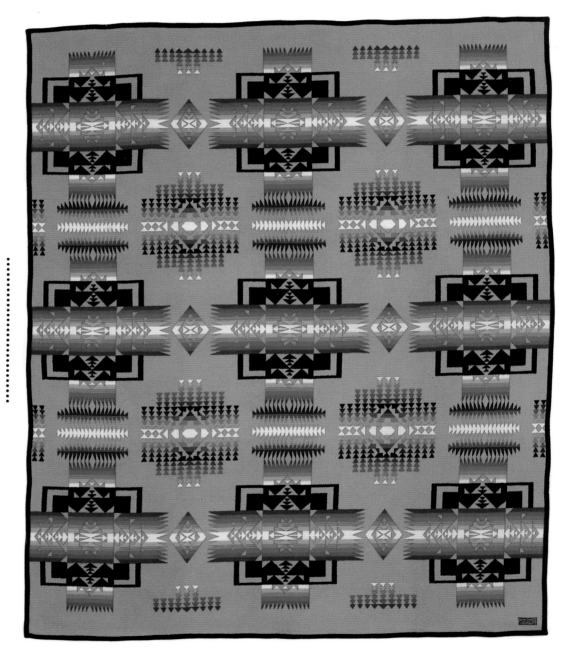

NINE ELEMENT CHIEF
JOSEPH ROBE, FIRST
INTRODUCED IN 1930
AND UNTIL 1952
PRODUCED IN ONLY
FOUR COLORS: LIGHT
TAN, TURQUOISE,
WHITE, AND TAN.
STILL IN PRODUCTION
TODAY IN 21 COLORS.

Pendleton - Virgin Wool

Blackfoot and Cayuse Indian Blankets and Shawls

Blackfoot
Color 5

IN PATTERNS and colors that have made "Pendletons" famous, but of lower quality, are the Blackfoot and Cayuse Indian Blankets and Shawls, some of which are pictured on this page.

Blackfoot Indian Blankets, felt bound, 62x76, and Shawls, yarn fringed, 62x66, are made in a wide range of colors and patterns. Order by color listed here and illustrated on Plate 1, opposite page:

No. 0—Red   No. 6—White
No. 1—Blue   No. 7—Pink
No. 2—Green   No. 8—Grey
No. 3—Purple   No. 9—Brown
No. 4—Magenta   No. 11—Olive Mix.
No. 5—Black   No. 12—Tan

THE CAYUSE Indian Shawl shown here gives an idea of the rich colors that are woven into even the lower priced products of Pendleton looms. With yarn fringe all around, Cayuse Shawls are made in body colors as listed above and illustrated on Plate 1, opposite page. Size 64x64. Blanket, felt bound, 62x74.

Cayuse
Color 0

[14]

CAYUSE/BLACKFOOT
PAGE FROM 1924
CATALOG.

BLACKFOOT
BANDED ROBE,
BLACKFOOT LABEL. ◄

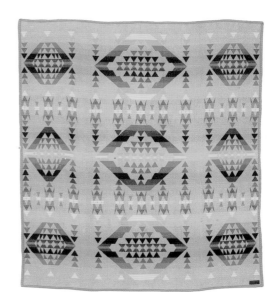

CAYUSE CENTER
POINT ROBE, REG.
CAYUSE LABEL. ►

CAYUSE OVERALL ROBE,
COPYRIGHT 1921 LABEL. ◄

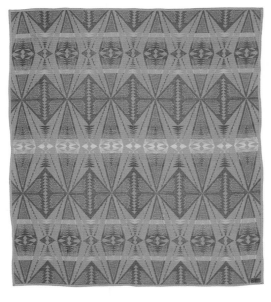

CAYUSE NINE ELEMENT
ROBE, COPYRIGHT
1921 LABEL. ►

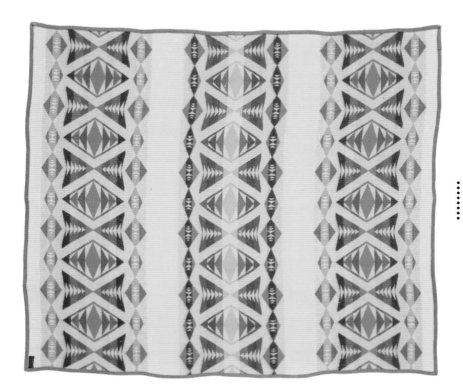

CAYUSE BANDED
ROBE, REG.
CAYUSE LABEL.

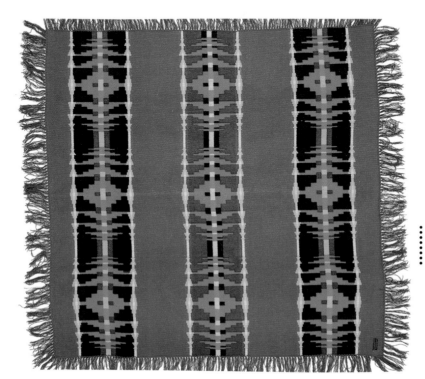

CAYUSE BANDED
SHAWL, PRE-1921
LABEL.

CAYUSE NINE
ELEMENT SHAWL,
REG. CAYUSE LABEL.

CAYUSE BANDED
ROBE, REG.
1921 LABEL.

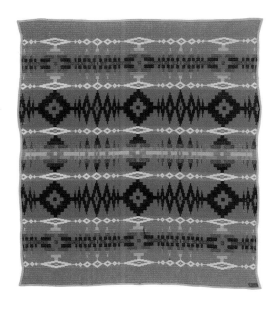

◀
CAYUSE BANDED ROBE,
COPYRIGHT 1921 LABEL.

▶
CAYUSE BANDED ROBE,
REG. CAYUSE LABEL.

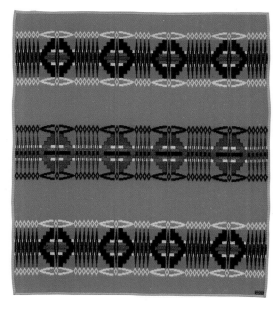

◀
CAYUSE NINE ELEMENT
ROBE, REG. CAYUSE
LABEL.

▶
CAYUSE BANDED ROBE,
PRE-1921 LABEL.

CAYUSE NINE ELEMENT
ROBE, COPYRIGHT
1921 LABEL.

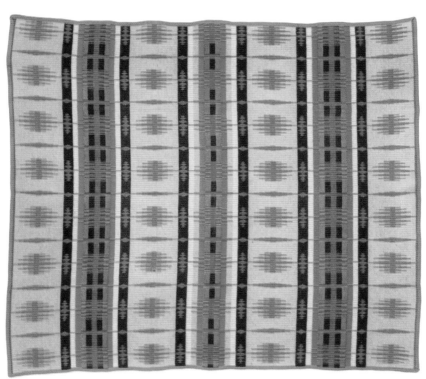

CAYUSE BANDED
ROBE, COPYRIGHT
1921 LABEL.

◄ CAYUSE BANDED ROBE, REG. CAYUSE LABEL.

► CAYUSE NINE ELEMENT ARROWHEAD ROBE, REG. CAYUSE LABEL.

◄ BLACKFOOT NINE ELEMENT ROBE, C. 1924, GREEN/BLACK BLACKFOOT LABEL.

► CAYUSE BANDED ROBE, REG. CAYUSE LABEL.

OREGON CITY HAPPY HUNTING GROUND ROBE, C. 1910–20. THE
DESIGN OF THIS ROBE WAS INTENDED TO REPRESENT THE INDIAN'S
DREAM OF THE HAPPY HUNTING GROUND.

NOVELTY DESIGNS
AND DUPLICATION OF PATTERNS

UNLIKE THE BLANKETS OF UNKNOWN ORIGIN PICTURED IN THE NEXT CHAPTER, THE BLANKETS WITH NOVELTY DESIGNS CAN OFTEN BE TRACED TO A SPECIFIC MANUFACTURER. HOWEVER, THEY DO NOT FIT IN WITH ANY OF THE GENERAL PATTERNS ATTRIBUTABLE TO THAT MANUFACTURER OR TO THE OVERALL TRADE BLANKET MARKET. TWO UNIQUE DESIGNS, THE HAPPY HUNTING GROUND DESIGN BLANKET AND THE TOTEM POLE DESIGN BLANKET, WERE PRODUCED BY THE OREGON CITY WOOLEN MILLS. OREGON CITY ALSO PRODUCED SPECIAL COMMEMORATIVE DESIGNS FOR THE SHRINE TEMPLE AND THE ELKS LODGE. • PENDLETON SET UP A SEPARATE COMPANY, THE CAYUSE BLANKET COMPANY, TO ORGANIZE AND SERVICE FUND-RAISING PROGRAMS FOR FRATERNAL ORGANIZATIONS, INCLUDING THE ELKS AND SHRINE. THE COMPANY PRODUCED THE COMMEMORATIVE BLANKETS WITH THE INSIGNIA OF THESE ORGANIZATIONS; BUT THE FUND DRIVES WERE NOT LIMITED TO THE SALE OF THE SPECIALTY BLANKETS AND INCLUDED ALL THE COMPANY'S DIFFERENT DESIGNS. • IN OTHER CASES, THERE WAS A DUPLICATION OF PATTERNS FROM ONE COMPANY TO ANOTHER. IN SUCH CASES, DETAILS OF MANUFACTURE OR SPECIFIC INFORMATION ARE THE ONLY WAY THAT A BLANKET CAN BE DEFINITELY ATTRIBUTED TO A SPECIFIC ORIGIN. BECAUSE OF THE COMPETITION BETWEEN OREGON CITY AND PENDLETON, THERE ARE SEVERAL EXAMPLES OF near duplication of patterns in blankets produced by these two companies.

In their marketing materials, the major trade blanket manufacturing firms acknowledged the competition in general terms about quality and authenticity but did not mention pattern duplication specifically. However, one Pendleton catalog reads:

True, many Pendleton designs have been copied through the years. However, the resultant prestige of continued high

OSAGE WOMEN C. 1890s. THE WOMAN ON THE RIGHT IS WEARING A BLANKET LIKE THE ONE SHOWN ON THE FACING PAGE. (PHOTO COURTESY WESTERN HISTORY COLLECTIONS, UNIVERSITY OF OKLAHOMA LIBRARY)

quality manufacturing standards and an understanding interpretation of the Indian's needs has provided Pendleton with the unique position of being identified in the minds of both the Indian and the White man as the exclusive manufacturer of Indian design blankets, robes, and shawls.

One of the popular Pendleton designs that was produced in a similar blanket by Oregon City Woolen Mills was the Tepee pattern (see page 161.) The Pendleton Tepee pattern, one of the company's most successful, is a banded design blanket with alternating bands—one band of complex terraced geometric designs followed by a band of four tepees. An example of the Tepee pattern, dated 1910, shows the two tepees in the center of each band placed base to base and the outer two tepees positioned so that their base is next to the top of the tepee at the center. The tepee elements are spaced so that each edge of the band has a part of the top of a tepee showing on the blanket.

The Oregon City Tepee pattern, dated approximately 1921, is similar to the Pendleton Tepee pattern in that it is a banded blanket with the wider bands consisting of complex geometric designs alternating with bands of four tepees. The Oregon City design is different in that the geometric design bands are wider and the tepee bands show four complete tepees, without the partial tepee design elements on each end of the band. To explain the difference in simple terms, the Oregon City design is an enlarged version of

the Pendleton design. There are other differences between the two designs. For example, the four tepees in the Oregon City blanket are positioned base to base—differently than the tepees in the Pendleton design. Either way, the Oregon City Tepee design is

very definitely derived from the same design as that for the Pendleton Tepee pattern. The question of whether this duplication is based on one designer working for Oregon City Woolen Mills copying the work of a designer working for Pendleton Woolen Mills cannot be answered.

FEATHER AND PIPE ROBE. C. 1890–1900. MANUFACTURER UNKNOWN.

OREGON CITY
CHILD'S COWBOY AND
INDIAN PICTORIAL
ROBE, C. 1920.

◄ OREGON CITY
PANAMA PACIFIC
INTERNATIONAL
EXPOSITION
BLANKET, 1915.

▶ OREGON CITY
LET ER BUCK
ROBE, C. 1910.

◄ OREGON CITY ELKS ROBE,
MANUFACTURED OVER
A NUMBER OF YEARS.
THIS ONE HAS A
POST-1921 LABEL.

▶ OREGON CITY MASONIC
BLANKET, DESIGNED
ESPECIALLY FOR
SHRINERS NATIONAL
CONVENTION IN
PORTLAND, JUNE 1920.

OREGON CITY
TOTEM POLE
ROBE, C. 1910.

◀ **PENDLETON BANDED ROBE, 1910 CATALOG.**

◀ **OREGON CITY BANDED ROBE, COVER OF 1911 CATALOG.**

▶ **PENDLETON CENTER POINT ROBE, 1921 LABEL.**

▶ **OREGON CITY CENTER POINT ROBE, 1926 CATALOG.**

"THE DRUMMER,"
C. 1911. THIS HOPI
MAN IS WEARING AN
OREGON CITY TEPEE
ROBE. (PHOTO BY H. F.
ROBINSON, COURTESY
MUSEUM OF NEW
MEXICO, NEG. 82778)

 OREGON CITY TEPEE
BLANKET, CA. 1920s.
NOTE THE DIAMOND
BOXES SEPARATING
THE TEPEE BASES.

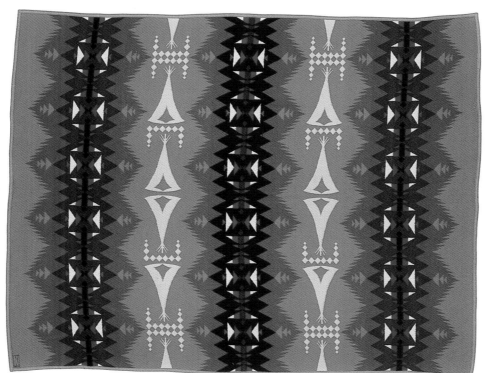

PENDLETON TEPEE
BLANKET, 1910–30s.
THIS WAS ONE OF
THE MOST POPULAR
BLANKETS PRODUCED
BY THE PENDLETON
WOOLEN MILLS.

161

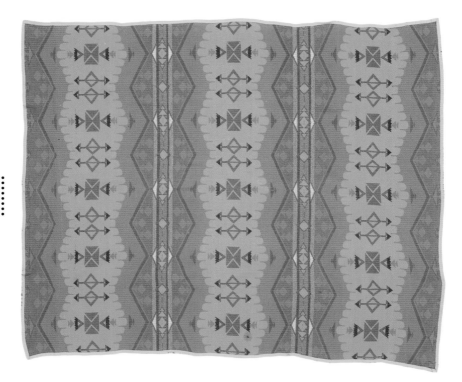

OREGON CITY
BANDED ROBE,
C. 1920s.

PENDLETON CAYUSE
BANDED ROBE,
C. 1920–30s.

BOW/ARROW AND
TOMAHAWK SHAWL,
MANUFACTURER
UNKNOWN. NOTE THE
FOUR DIFFERENT
COLORS OF FRINGE.

BANDED STAR AND CRESCENT SHAWL, C. 1900–20s.

AMERICAN INDIAN TRADE BLANKETS OF UNKNOWN ORIGIN

THERE WERE UNDOUBTEDLY SEVERAL COMPANIES THAT HAVE CONTINUED TO OPERATE IN ANONYMITY BECAUSE THEY DID NOT ADVERTISE OR DEVELOP LABELS FOR THE BLANKETS THEY PRODUCED. THESE "UNKNOWN" BLANKETS ARE GENERALLY SIMILAR TO THE BLANKETS PRODUCED BY THE MAJOR COMPANIES IN THAT THEY ARE MANUFACTURED IN A SIMILAR WAY AND OFTEN INCLUDE MANY OF THE DESIGN ELEMENTS THAT ARE MUCH THE SAME AS THE BLANKETS PRODUCED BY THE MAJOR COMPANIES. IN NAVAJO WEAVING, WEAVINGS THAT CONTAIN CHARACTERISTIC DESIGNS FROM MORE THAN ONE AREA OF THE RESERVATION ARE CALLED "GENERAL AREA" WEAVINGS. SPECIFYING THE ORIGIN OF THE UNKNOWN TRADE BLANKETS IS RATHER LIKE TRACING THE IDENTITY OF A GENERAL AREA NAVAJO WEAVING. • IT IS DIFFICULT TO DETERMINE DETAILS OF DESIGN AND MANUFACTURE THAT MIGHT IDENTIFY THE BLANKET AS THE PRODUCT OF ONE MANUFACTURER OR ANOTHER. ONE CAN CHECK LOCAL LIBRARIES FOR BACKGROUND ON LOCAL MANUFACTURERS OR DETERMINE AN INDIVIDUAL BLANKET'S PROVENANCE THROUGH SALES RECORDS. GENERALLY, A COMPARISON TO OTHER BLANKETS, LIKE THOSE ILLUSTRATED IN THIS BOOK, IS THE MOST EFFECTIVE MEANS OF DETERMINING A PROBABLE IDENTITY FOR A TRADE BLANKET OF UNKNOWN ORIGIN. SOMETIMES THIS SLEUTHING PAYS OFF WITH AN IDENTITY FOR THE BLANKET FROM AN UNKNOWN MANUFACTURER. IN OTHER CASES, THE HISTORICAL CONTEXT FOR AN UNKNOWN BLANKET CAN BE ESTABLISHED BY IDENTIFYING THE BLANKET IN A HISTORIC PHOTOGRAPH.

JUANITA ESTRELLA
AND GENEVIEVE PECOS
AT THE COCHITI
PUEBLO, C. 1920s,
WEARING A STAR AND
CRESCENT SHAWL.
(PHOTO COURTESY
MUSEUM OF NEW
MEXICO, NEG. 106887)

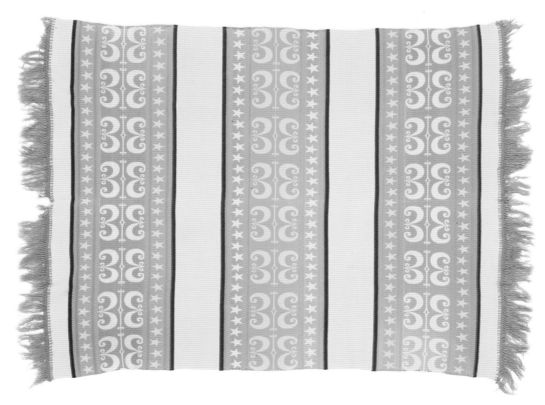

BANDED STAR AND
CRESCENT SHAWL,
C. 1900–20s.

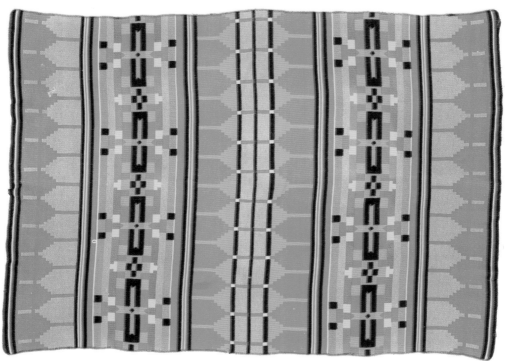

THIS BANDED ROBE
IS POSSIBLY AN
EARLY BUELL, BASED
ON THE BINDING.

BANDED OSAGE ROBE.
THIS STYLE OF BLANKET
WAS INTRODUCED
THROUGH THE OSAGE
MERCANTILE COMPANY
AROUND THE 1890s AND
IS BELIEVED TO HAVE
BEEN MANUFACTURED
IN GERMANY.

TOMAHAWK PICTORIAL CENTER POINT ROBE, C. 1900–20s.

STAR AND DIAMOND BANDED ROBE, C. 1900–20.

ROUND CORNER ROBE, C. 1890–1900s.

BANDED SHAWL, C. 1900–20s.

169

BANDED
CROSS ROBE,
C. 1900–20.

BANDED
FLOWER SHAWL,
C. 1900–20.

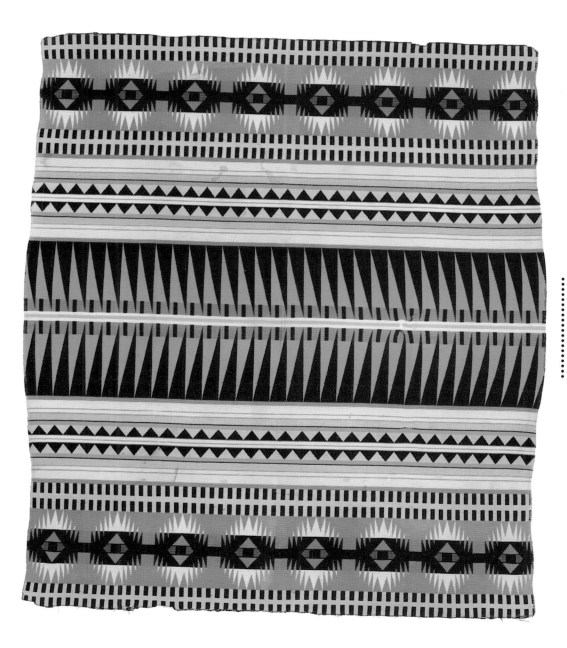

MULTI-DESIGN
(BACKGAMMON)
ROBE, C. 1890–1900s.
THE UNIQUE ASPECT
OF THIS BLANKET IS
THE USE OF MANY
DESIGN ELEMENTS.

SOUTHWEST TRAILS™ "CHIHUAHUA TRAIL"™ BLANKET WAS
MADE IN 1992 IN A NUMBERED 1,000 EDITION IN ULTRASUEDE
BINDING AND AN UNNUMBERED OPEN EDITION IN WOOL FELT
BINDING AND NAPPED. (DESIGN © 1992 RAMONA
SAKIESTEWA, PHOTO COURTESY RAY DEWEY)

CONTEMPORARY COLLECTIBLE BLANKETS

IN 1992, THE MARKET FOR AMERICAN INDIAN TRADE BLANKETS INCLUDES FOUR IMPORTANT COMPONENTS: (1) THE AMERICAN INDIAN CUSTOMERS WHO CONTINUE TO USE BLANKETS (AND SHAWLS) IN TRADITIONAL WAYS; (2) COLLECTORS OF HISTORIC TRADE BLANKETS; (3) COLLECTORS OF COMMEMORATIVE, LIMITED-EDITION BLANKETS; AND (4) THE MARKET FOR TRADE BLANKETS AS INTERIOR DESIGN ACCESSORIES. • PENDLETON WOOLEN MILLS IS THE ONLY COMPANY THAT CONTINUES TO MANUFACTURE TRADE BLANKETS TO SUPPLY BOTH THE AMERICAN INDIAN MARKET AND THE COLLECTOR MARKET FOR COMMEMORATIVE AND LIMITED-EDITION BLANKETS. EVEN THOUGH THE CATALOG OF STANDARD DESIGNS OFFERED BY THE COMPANY HAS BEEN REDUCED DRAMATICALLY SINCE WORLD WAR II, THE BLANKETS STILL ARE USED AS WEARING BLANKETS AND FOR GIFTS AMONG THE TRADITIONAL NATIVE AMERICAN PEOPLE THROUGHOUT THE COUNTRY. PENDLETON SELLS MORE THAN ONE-HALF OF ITS TOTAL BLANKET PRODUCTION TO CUSTOMERS ON THE RESERVATIONS, AND THE COMPANY'S PRODUCTION IS INCREASING. SINCE AMERICAN INDIAN PEOPLE ARE MORE MOBILE THAN EVER BEFORE, THEY NO LONGER BUY THE BLANKETS EXCLUSIVELY FROM TRADING POSTS, BUT MAKE THE TRIP INTO CITIES AND TOWNS NEAR THEIR TRIBAL LANDS WHERE THEY BUY THE PENDLETON BLANKETS FROM RETAILERS OF ALL KINDS.

Another aspect of the American Indian trade blanket market that has developed recently is the market for commemorative, limited-edition blankets. Commemorative blankets like the "Harding" pattern or the "Chief Joseph" pattern have been produced for decades, but the limited-edition blanket is new in the last five years. With the limited-edition market has come a renewed appreciation for the trade blanket as art object. The commemorative blanket encourages a stronger awareness of the history of trade blankets. For example, several of the recent commemorative limited editions have been issued by the historic trading posts of the Southwest. Among the posts which have released commemorative limited-edition blankets is

Babbitt Brothers General Merchants, The Hubbell Trading Post, and the Cameron Trading Post. Each blanket edition (Babbitt Brothers has now issued four editions) exhibits a distinctive design that is tied to the specific trading post.

In addition to building an awareness and understanding of the trade blanket's history, Pendleton has also used the commemorative blankets to build awareness of tribes outside the major trade blanket markets of the Southwest and the Northwest. For example, in developing the Sioux Star pattern blanket, the manager of Pendleton's blanket division, Bill Nance, traveled to Sioux country in South Dakota to research designs and color preferences. For another commemorative edition, the

LEFT: HUBBELL TRADING POST, 1990, EDITION WAS 1,000. RIGHT: CAMERON TRADING POST 75TH ANNIVERSARY, EDITION WAS 250 WITH GOLD LABELS AND 750 WITH SILVER LABELS. CENTER: BABBITT TRADING COMPANY, 1990, EDITION WAS 2,000. (THE OTHER BABBITT BLANKETS ARE A 1989 100TH ANNIVERSARY EDITION OF 1,000 QUANTITY, A 1991 EDITION OF 2,000 QUANTITY, AND A 1992 EDITION OF 1,000 QUANTITY.)

Iroquois turtle design, Pendleton hired a Native American artist to work on the design development.

Another Native American artist, Ramona Sakiestewa, has created a series of unique designs, six of which will be used for limited-edition blankets that will commemorate Southwestern Trails—The Santa Fe Trail,™ The Chihuahua Trail,™ The Chaco Trail,™ The Hopi Trail,™ The Iron Horse Trail,™ and The Navajo Trail.™ Sakiestewa is working with the Dewey Trading Company™ in Santa Fe to develop the Southwest Trails™ commemorative blankets. The blankets will be manufactured by Pendleton and marketed by Dewey Trading Company.™

While the commemorative editions have heightened the market for trade blankets as art objects, a growing appreciation of the blanket designs has built a market for blankets as interior design accessories. The blankets are used as bedspreads, couch covers, and wall hangings, just as the trade blanket companies advertised in the early decades of the twentieth century when they were developing a non-Indian market for the blankets.

The diversification of the trade blanket market indicates a steadily growing interest in the history and in the colorful designs of all types of trade blankets. This diversification also represents an opportunity for anyone to learn more about trade blankets, whether as a serious collector, as a historian, or to simply enjoy the beauty and craft of the American Indian trade blanket.

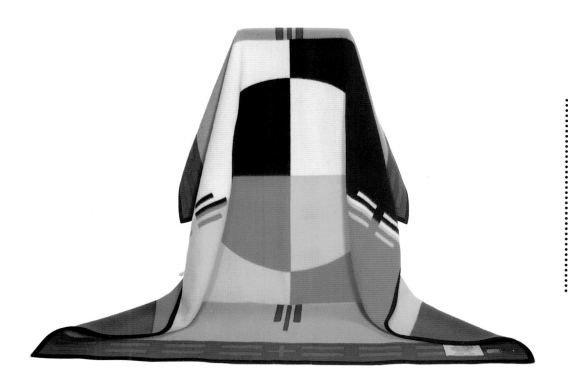

"ELDERS" ROBE REPRESENTS THE FOUR STAGES OF LIFE. MANUFACTURED BY PENDLETON WOOLEN MILLS IN 1992; THE FIRST 300 BLANKETS ARE NUMBERED AND THE REST IS AN OPEN EDITION. (PHOTO COURTESY PENDLETON WOOLEN MILLS)

ALL THREE BLANKETS
ARE PENDLETONS.
LEFT TO RIGHT:
IROQUOIS
CONFEDERACY
TURTLE, 1991;
POTLATCH, 1990;
SIOUX STAR, 1989.
THE FIRST THREE
HUNDRED BLANKETS
PRODUCED WERE
NUMBERED, THEN
THE BLANKETS WERE
OFFERED IN AN
OPEN EDITION.

BABBITTS' "NAVAJO
STORM SERIES" 1992
LIMITED EDITION
WAS MODELED ON
AN ORIGINAL NAVAJO
WOVEN BLANKET.
MADE IN AN EDITION
OF 1,000. (PHOTO
COURTESY BABBITS)

THE "SANTA FE TRAIL"™
BLANKET WAS
PRODUCED IN A
LIMITED EDITION OF
2,000 IN 1991 WITH
SPECIAL BINDING,
THEN IN AN OPEN EDI-
TION. IT USES CLASSIC
PUEBLO ELEMENTS
FROM AN EARLY
PENDLETON DESIGN
AND HONORS THE
TRADITION OF TRADE
ROUTES IN THE WEST.
(DESIGN © 1992
RAMONA SAKIESTEWA,
PHOTO COURTESY
RAY DEWEY)

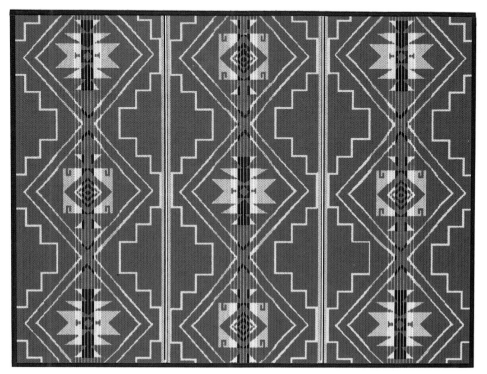

THE "CHACO TRAIL"™
BLANKET WAS ISSUED
IN 1992 IN LIMITED
EDITION OF 1,000
WITH SPECIAL
BINDING, PLUS AN
OPEN EDITION
NAPPED AND FELT-
BOUND. WATER
CLAN SYMBOLS OF
CLOUDS AND RAIN
COMMEMORATE THE
PREHISTORIC VILLAGES
OF THE ANASAZI AND
THE WEB OF TRAILS
THAT CONNECTED
THEM. (DESIGN © 1992
RAMONA SAKIESTEWA
PHOTO COURTESY
RAY DEWEY)

BIBLIOGRAPHY

Amsden, Charles Avery. *Navaho Weaving: Its Technique and Its History*. Glorieta, N.M.: The Rio Grande Press, 1934.

The Works of Hubert Howe Bancroft Volume XXVII of History of the Northwest Coast, Vol. I (1543–1800). San Francisco,: A. L. Bancroft and Co., 1884.

Davidson, Gordon Charles, *The North West Company*. Berkeley: University of California Press, 1918.

Davison's Textile Blue Book, 40th annual edition, July 1927 to July 1928. New York City: Davison, 1927.

Dedera, Don. *Navajo Rugs: How to Find, Evaluate, Buy and Care for Them*. Foreword by Clay Lockett. Flagstaff, Az.: Northland Press, 1975.

Dockham's American Report and Directory of the Textile Manufacture and Dry Goods Trade, 1891–92, 13th ed. Manchester, Eng.: C. A. Dockham and Co., 1891.

Early, Patrick. *Lecture on The History of the Witney Blanket Industry*. London: The Royal Society of Arts and the Department of Education of the International Wool Secretariat, 1956.

Hail, Barbara A. *Hau, Kola! The Plains Indian Collection of the Haffenreffer Museum of Anthropology*. Providence, R.I.: Haffenreffer Museum of Anthropology, Brown University, 1980.

Kent, Kate Peck. *Pueblo Indian Textiles: A Living Tradition*. Santa Fe, N. M.: School of American Research Press, 1983.

Lomax, Alfred L. *Pioneer Woolen Mills in Oregon: A History of Wool and the Woolen Textile Industry in Oregon, 1811–1875*. Portland, Ore.: Binfords and Mort, 1941.

_____. *Later Woolen Mills in Oregon: A History of the Woolen Mills Which Followed the Pioneer Mills*. Portland, Ore.: Binfords and Mort, 1974.

MacKay, Douglas. *The Honourable Company: A History of Hudson's Bay Company*. New York City: Bobbs-Merrill Co., 1936.

Frank McNitt. *The Indian Traders*. Norman: University of Oklahoma Press, 1962.

Morrow, Mable. *Indian Rawhide: An American Folk Art*. Norman: University of Oklahoma Press, 1975.

Pendleton Woolen Mills Catalog, reproduction of the original Pendleton catalog from 1912. Albuquerque, New Mexico. Avanyu Publishing, Inc., 1987.

Powell, Peter John. *People of the Sacred Mountain: A History of the Northern Cheyenne Chiefs and Warrior Societies, 1830–1879. With an Epilogue 1969–1794. Two Volumes*. San Francisco: Harper and Row, 1981.

Report on Indians Taxed and Not Taxed, 1890 Census Bureau.

Rodee, Marian E. *Old Navajo Rugs: Their Development from 1900 to 1940, with Keys to Their Identification*. Albuquerque: University of New Mexico Press, 1981.

_____. *Weaving of the Southwest*. West Chester, Penn.: Schiffer, 1987.

Shields, G. O. *The Blanket Indian of the Northwest*. New York: Vechten Waring Co., 1921

Statistics of Woollen Manufactories in the United States, by the Proprietor of the Condensing Card Wm. H. Graham, New York, 1845.

Tripp, Clare Ketchum. *Origin, Organization and Operation of the Pendleton Woolen Mills*. Seattle: Washington-Oregon Industries Education Bureau, 1928.

United States Textile Manufacturer's Directory. Boston: National Association of Wool Manufacturers, Boston, 1874.

World's Fair Edition of *The Blue Book Textile Directory of the United States and Canada*, Seventeenth Annual Edition, 1904–1905. 1904, Davison Publishing Company, New York.

ENDNOTES

CHAPTER 2

1. Hail, p. 38.

2. Ibid.

3. Shields, p. 211.

4. Ibid.

5. Ibid.

6. Amsden, p. 103.

7. Rodee, p. 2.

8. Powell, p. 116

CHAPTER 3

1. Powell, p. 354.

2. Mackay, p. 48.

3. Mackay, pp. 36–37.

4. Bancroft, p. 466–67

5. Ibid., p.458

6. Ibid.

7. Early, p. 13.

CHAPTER 4

1. Dedera, p. 33

2. McNitt, p. 222.

3. Ibid.

CHAPTER 5

1. Lomax, p. 99.

CHAPTER 11

1. McNitt, p. 222.

2. Ibid.